Storms *and* Flames *of* Glory

Storms *and* Flames *of* Glory

E. C. Nakeli

King's Word Publishing

© 2016 by E.C. Nakeli

Published by King's Word Publication

For your questions and publishing needs, write to:

    E.C. Nakeli
    40 S Church St
    Westminster, MD 21157
    E-mail: *ecnakeli@yahoo.com*

Printed in the United States of America

All rights reserved. No part of this publication may be reproduced, stored in a retrieval systems, or transmitted in ay form or by any means— for example, electronic, photocopy, recording—without the prior written permission of the publisher. The only exception is brief quotations in printed reviews.

E.C. Nakeli

To contact the author, write to:

    CMFI
    40 S Church St
    Westminster, MD 21157
    E-mail: *ecnakeli@yahoo.com*

Storms and Flames of Glory 1 - Final Compilation 2/ E.C. Nakeli

ISBN: 978-1-945055-02-7

    Unless otherwise indicated, Scriptures references are from
    THE HOLY BIBLE, NEW INTERNATIONAL VERSION®, NIV®
    Copyright © 1973, 1978, 1984, 2011 by Biblica, Inc™
    Used by permission. All rights reserved worlwide.

Cover and Interior Design: Zach Essama

Table of Contents

Table of Content v
Aknowledgements vii
Dedication ix
Part one: The Life of Joseph 1
Chapter 1: Pregnant with Vision 3
Chapter 2: The Storm 7
Chapter 3: Trials in the Storm 15
Chapter 4: Through the Storm to Glory 25
Chapter 5: A Persistent Storm 31
Part Two: The Life of Job 39
Chapter 6: Successful and Secure 41
Chapter 7: The Place of Worship 49
Chapter 8: Relationships: A Peril or a Blessing? 55
Chapter 9: Holding Fast 69
Part Three: The Life of Jeremiah 75
Chapter 10: Where He Came From 77
Chapter 11: Hypocrites in the House 85
Chapter 12: A Renewed Trust 97
Part Four: Lessons in the Storms (Why Storms?) 105
Chapter 13: A Call to Suffer 107
Chapter 14: Avoiding Unnecessary Storms 117
Chapter 15: Reasons for the Storms 125
Chapter 16: Facing the Storm 137
Chapter 16: God's Deliverance 151
Chapter 18: The Glory of the Storm 161
Chapter 19: A Friend's Testimony 173
Conclusion 183

Aknowledgements

I will like to acknowledge the support of the following people who gave some special assistance for this book to reach its final stage:

I want to say thank you to Clovis Ebage who did the typing of the manuscript.

I want to also thank mummy Grace Epamba who did the first proofreading of the manuscript.

Finally I wish to say thank you to all those who supported this project spiritually and morally. Your reward is great; both in this life and in the one to come.

A special acknowledgment goes to my dear friend Gabila Fohtung for his willingness to be a blessing to the readers. God bless your heart.

Dedication

This book is dedicated to my beloved daughters in the Lord, Bernadette and Tessa who through the storms and flames have learned to trust and rely on the Lord; the One they love with all their hearts. I saw you both brave it through those difficult days and storms wholeheartedly holding to the Lord who could carry through. I am proud of you. This book is also dedicated to all those who are going through storms in their lives. May the Almighty King of kings and LORD of lords use it to bless you and bring a renewed hope and confidence in your hearts so that you may see the glory that lies beyond every high and stormy gale.

Part One

The Life of Joseph

Many people are familiar with the story of Joseph as it is often recounted in Sunday schools or in Religious Studies classes, especially in Christian schools. For instance before I became versed with the Bible, I could give an account of what befell Joseph and draw my own conclusions. I believe this story of Joseph has much to teach us than the average mind can grasp.

Many people may just view it as a *"Bible Comedy"*. These few Bible chapters on the life of Joseph contain enormous spiritual truth and insight for those who go beyond the surface of the narrative. In fact through the story, God can reveal to us some very vital spiritual lessons which cannot be drawn from any other Bible passage. For this reason, I invite you to join me in this sail through *"Storms and Flames of Glory"*, as we study the lives of Joseph, Job, and Jeremiah, using it as a mirror to see ourselves, see where we have *"fallen short of God's grace"* and implore His mercy and compassion.

May these lessons be written on the tablet of your heart by the Spirit of truth, with ink as red as the blood of the *"Lamb that was slain"*, for only then shall it be permanent, for revision and for lasting impact in your life and in the lives of others.

Chapter One

Pregnant With Vision

Dreams And Wishes

> *"Joseph, a young man of seventeen, was tending the flocks with his brothers, the sons of Bilhah and the sons of Zilpah, his father's wives, and he brought their father a bad report about them. Now Israel loved Joseph more than any of his other sons, because he had been born to him in his old age; and he made a richly ornamented robe for him. When his brothers saw that their father loved him more than any of them, they hated him and could not speak a kind word to him"* (Genesis 37:1-4).

Just as a reminder to us, Joseph was the first son of his mother in a polygamous home, the eleventh son of his father and the twelfth child in the family. He was much of a blessing to his mother as he was conceived many years after marriage. He came at a time when the mother had given up all hopes of bringing forth a baby from her own womb, though she was more loved than her mate, also her sister.

In a sense, Joseph was treated as the first son by Jacob, since he was the first son of the woman he loved so dearly and could lay down his life for. Fourteen years of hard work just to get a wife! Many of us will give up after the third year. As the first son of the mother of two, Joseph was an object of love to both father and mother; he was indeed a blessed child. This is an overview of who Joseph was in his family.

Many people's lives are filled with dreams, wishes, hopes and aspirations. Many youngsters have been given promises by their parents, siblings or external relatives. The world around them has much to offer. They have many ambitions and the future appears bright and promising. Many of them hope for a happy and comfortable life. We dream to rise to heights in *"Christian Stardom"* and be the *"talk of our generation"*. Often there are several reasons for such hopes and dreams. For after all we rely on the promises of God as understood from scripture. We want to be at the top and never at the bottom (Deuteronomy 28), we want all *"our needs"* to be met (Philippians 4:19), we expect nothing but prosperity, a good future (Jeremiah 29:11).

Yes! God has promised us a future – a bright future. He has promised to prosper us, so in our finite thinking, all that comes our way must be *"good"* according to our understanding of goodness. So we dread suffering, failure and all that appears negative – most often that which hurts our pride and ego. Like Joseph, we have dreams we wish will come true and may be, genuinely, these dreams are from the *"Revealer of mysteries"* and so we have every reason to believe in them and long to have them realized (Vs 3).

Like Joseph, many a youngster is from a home in which he is the object of attraction of the family. Deeply loved and cherished both by friends and relatives. So much has been and is being invested in us, thus we do not want to disappoint or give reasons for them to regret their confidence. So we are ready to do anything to succeed. We want to prove our worth and give them more reasons for future confidence in us. We hope to be the one whose *"sheaf rose and stood upright"* and dream to the see *"the sun and moon and eleven stars bowing down to me"*. With such *"vision"* we live with an utmost determination to overcome all obstacles and accomplish our dreams. For the dreams build in us a super driving force which nothing can resist. The tides act in favor of our dreams and it seems all we need to do is just relax in the current and be carried to our destination.

The staircase to success, made of gold, decorated with diamonds and roses is before us and we are determined to climb to the very top of it. Sooner or later, we realize in dismay that it is not the true picture of life and of success. We are awakened to see that life is not just a fairy tale and that indeed we have been in a fantasy world. We come to see that the staircase to success is not in any way made of gold or surrounded by roses and diamonds. We come to see that though roses may be at the top, the staircase is full of thorns that pierce us and rocks which cause us to stumble and obtain unanticipated bruises and hurts and failures and disappointments. We come to realize what we thought would be made of gold, was instead made of tar, which sticks to our feet, stain our cloths and hinder our smooth motion.

One more lesson to draw from here. Have you a dream? Do not expect that all around you would be in favor of that dream. Some would outrightly oppose you and others would nurse secret wishes to see you fail; some would even make soulish prayers. It was the case with Joseph, those who opposed his dream were his own very brothers whom in every sense would have been the ones to support and encourage him to press on.

How often do those we love betray us when we need them most! How often we stretch our hands with no one to hold them and pull us forth. Do not fret, there is someone amongst the multitudes who has kept your dream in mind and longs to see you attain them, and may be without your knowledge is praying and holding on God to see it fulfilled. It maybe your father, like in Joseph's case, your mother, a brother, a sister, or a friend. What are your dreams? Do not hesitate to share them; there is at least someone to stand with you, at least one who is not going to be in the camp of your opposers.

Chapter Two

The Storm

"Now his brothers had gone to graze their father's flocks near Shechem, and Israel said to Joseph, 'As you know, your brothers are grazing the flocks near Shechem. Come, I am going to send you to them.' 'Very well,' he replied. So he said to him, 'Go and see if all is well with your brothers and with the flocks, and bring word back to me.' Then he sent him off from the Valley of Hebron. When Joseph arrived at Shechem, a man found him wandering around in the fields and asked him, 'What are you looking for?' He replied, 'I'm looking for my brothers. Can you tell me where they are grazing their flocks?' 'They have moved on from here,' the man answered. 'I heard them say, "Let's go to Dothan."' So Joseph went after his brothers and found them near Dothan. But they saw him in the distance, and before he reached them, they plotted to kill him. 'Here comes that dreamer!' they said to each other. 'Come now, let's kill him and throw him into one of these cisterns and say that a ferocious animal devoured him. Then we'll see what comes of his dreams.' When Reuben heard this, he tried to rescue him from their hands. 'Let's not take his life,' he said. 'Don't shed any blood. Throw him into this cistern here in the desert, but don't lay a hand on him.' Reuben said this to rescue him from them and take him back to his father. So when Joseph came to his brothers, they stripped him of his robe—the richly ornamented robe he was wearing- and they took him and threw him into the cistern. Now the cistern was empty; there was no water in it. As they sat down to eat their

meal, they looked up and saw a caravan of Ishmaelites coming from Gilead. Their camels were loaded with spices, balm and myrrh, and they were on their way to take them down to Egypt. Judah said to his brothers, 'What will we gain if we kill our brother and cover up his blood? Come, let's sell him to the Ishmaelites and not lay our hands on him; after all, he is our brother, our own flesh and blood.' His brothers agreed. So when the Midianite merchants came by, his brothers pulled Joseph up out of the cistern and sold him for twenty shekels of silver to the Ishmaelites, who took him to Egypt. When Reuben returned to the cistern and saw that Joseph was not there, he tore his clothes. He went back to his brothers and said, 'The boy isn't there! Where can I turn now?' Then they got Joseph's robe, slaughtered a goat and dipped the robe in the blood. They took the ornamented robe back to their father and said, 'We found this. Examine it to see whether it is your son's robe.'

"*He recognized it and said, 'It is my son's robe! Some ferocious animal has devoured him. Joseph has surely been torn to pieces.' Then Jacob tore his clothes, put on sackcloth and mourned for his son many days. All his sons and daughters came to comfort him, but he refused to be comforted. 'No,' he said, 'in mourning will I go down to the grave to my son.' So his father wept for him. Meanwhile, the Midianites sold Joseph in Egypt to Potiphar, one of Pharaoh's officials, the captain of the guard*" (Genesis 37:12-36).

Joseph seems to have been the manager of his father's business. He was the one to go for business trips and supervise shepherds and the sheep. Those whose welfare he went to ensure saw him from afar and plotted to kill him. Have you been betrayed by the very people you have done all to help? You tried to seek the welfare of some people, you wandered in the desert, exposed to heat and cold only that you may find them and know how they fare yet all you got was rejection. Those for whom you risked your life cannot even appreciate your effort and kindness. All you get in return is hatred and conspiracy to bring you down?

At the height of Joseph's dreams came the unexpected journey to Egypt. Here is Joseph facing the threat of death in the hands of his own brothers. Those who should have offered him the protection he needed, conspired to take away his life. My brother, have you a dream? Do you know the enemies to that dream? You can know them by their attitude towards you. Ask the Lord to show you the enemies to your dream, those who are saying in their hearts, *"Do you intend to reign over us? Will you actually rule us?"* The purpose for this is not to treat them with contempt or hate or live in suspicion, but so you can love them and pray for them.

Beware of Dream Killers

Joseph's, brothers' target was not Joseph their younger brother but Joseph the vision bearer or dreamer. Their target was his dreams. When they saw him from afar, they did not say *"here comes Joseph"* but *"here comes the dreamer"*. Thus their hatred was towards the man with the dreams. Man, you better stay away from the enemies to your dream because if they have the opportunity they will do everything to kill the vision.

Many who had a vision or a dream from the Lord, who wanted to live fully for the Lord, ended up backsliding and dying spiritually. Why? Because they were in a company of people who were going nowhere, who subtly intoxicated their minds with cynical attitudes and in the long run they became lukewarm and useless in the hands of God. One thing is clear though: not all such enemies to vision can be identified. Some of them live in utter disguise as though they are in favor of your dream. Do not fret! In their company is one man who takes the side of God. In every band of opposers, there is a Reuben whom God shall use to alter their evil course, and rescue you. May God raise many Reubens in the camp of the enemy of His people. Someone shall rescue you and take you back to your father – the one who shares your dreams and vision.

Stripped of Your Identity?

Joseph was stripped off his coat of many colors that externally distinguished him from others and was thrown into the cistern to die. Have you been stripped off your ornamented robe and thrown into a cistern, a waterless cistern by the circumstances of life? You have been a *"victim to circumstances"* and now you are alone in that deep cistern with no hope of coming out, no sign of rescue in the horizon, no hand to pull you out, no voice to comfort you. Those responsible for your misfortune are out there celebrating while you sit in the cistern hungry and in torments. My brother, my sister though there is every reason for you to despair, there is one reason to have hope: there is a Father who knows you are there and is arranging for your rescue. The very people who sought your downfall will have to lift you out. God has not abandoned you. Remember Modecai and Haman: This is the kind of glorious deliverance God is preparing for you.

As earlier mentioned, at the height of Joseph's dreams, just when he had begun having control over his father's enterprise, he was spared from death and sold by his own brothers to unknown merchants. This was the beginning of an unknown journey into Egypt, a land he knew not, a land his father knew not, amongst a people of strange language and culture as a slave. Here is Joseph with all his dreams of a bright future, sold into the cruelty of slavery. What awaits a slave but endless suffering, hard labor, pains and probably very little to eat daily.

Humanly speaking, this was the end of Joseph's dreams and his career as manager of his father's enterprise. At such an instance, many of us will begin to wonder if we really dreamt what we announced. We doubt if the dream was really from God, if so then why this? Why that? We tend to see God's promises failing and in our folly we dare ask God why everything seems to work against our dreams, hopes, and wishes. May God have mercy on us! Often, we allow doubt to creep in and cripple us. We think we made a mistake, we think we are in the wrong path and often blame ourselves for the *"wrong choices"* forgetting to know that God's ways are very different from ours. He works in ways we cannot comprehend. He remains incomprehensible. But we carry on the load of despair and failure and we doubt if indeed God is really our Father. Do not fret, He is!

Let go of the idols

Let us shift our attention a bit from Joseph to someone passively involved. Jacob, the father of Joseph had worked so hard to have Rachael, Joseph's mother as his wife. She was the object of Jacob's love and attention but died in the prime of her life. He loved her in a special way, for he had invested so much in her. I believe the death of Rachael was a big blow to Jacob. God in His love for you and me seems always to take from us that which is the center of our affection. He seems to always strike at that which we hold to dearly and protect the most, or our very strength and achievement or what we have labored so dearly to obtain and hold in esteem apart from Him. Among the Patriarchs and their wives only Rachael was buried away from the common burial place. She died on the way to Bethlehem, the birthplace of deliverance for the human race.

Let this lesson sink deep down into your subconscious mind; <u>the road to the birthplace of deliverance shall bring death to all you cherish apart from the Savior.</u> After the death of Joseph's mother, the love Jacob had for her was not lost, it was transferred to Joseph who then *"inherited a double portion"* of his father's love. Have you realized that we often fail in the tests God passes us through? We often seem to find new things on which to place the love and attention, which we are supposed to give to the Lord.

God in His sovereignty had not finished with Jacob, so in His eternal plan for Joseph, He had to take away the delight of Jacob's eye. The lesson here is, <u>God will not surrender to us but will deal with us until He has finally worked out that which He wants to work in us and through us.</u> The more we corporate with Him in our storms of life, the more we progress in the school of Christlikeness. The more stubborn and stiff-necked we prove the more pain and bruises we incur.

This time, it was a bigger blow to Jacob. He did not lose only a son, but also the heir and manager of his enterprise, and the only one on whom he could rely for adequate and honest reports (for Benjamin was still very young). Jacob was having his lot, one problem after another directed to a specific target – the object of his love. One sad thing is that his other children were very dishonest; it is as if they sought their father's ruin. Are you a parent? Do you find your children hurting you in all they do?

They deceive you to meet their selfish ends, care nothing about your welfare and cannot even give any account of what you have entrusted to them. There is still hope. Do not despair; God is on your side. Through them He is working out something in you which no-one else can do. Trust God for the best out of it.

At this point in Jacob's life, the wound was so deep that he mourned for days – many days, who knows how long. He despaired even of comfort and of life and decided that in *"mourning will I go down to the grave to my son"*. Do you see the extent of his love for Joseph? He was ready to mourn till his dying day. He refused all comfort. At this point in time, one may conclude that Jacob had learned his lesson, but as we shall see later, this is not the case. He had failed this test too and needed a make-up test. What a gracious examiner God is. More on Jacob later!

God's Favor in The Storm

> *"Now Joseph had been taken down to Egypt. Potiphar, an Egyptian who was one of Pharaoh's officials, the captain of the guard, bought him from the Ishmaelites who had taken him there. The LORD was with Joseph and he prospered, and he lived in the house of his Egyptian master. 3 When his master saw that the LORD was with him and that the LORD gave him success in everything he did, 4 Joseph found favor in his eyes and became his attendant. Potiphar put him in charge of his household, and he entrusted to his care everything he owned. 5 From the time he put him in charge of his household and of all that he owned, the LORD blessed the household of the Egyptian because of Joseph. The blessing of the LORD was on everything Potiphar had, both in the house and in the field. 6 So he left in Joseph's care everything he had; with Joseph in charge, he did not concern himself with anything except the food he ate"* (Genesis 39:1-6a).

Whenever we are going through storms in the perfect will of our Father, God arranges our steps, places and people we will come in contact with. He goes right ahead of us to prepare the way so we can learn the most out of it, if only we trust and relax in Him. What encourages me most in this passage

Chapter 2: The Storm

is *"the Lord was with Joseph and he prospered"*. God, our Father, in His infinite love and mercy never abandons us in our problems, even the ones we bring upon ourselves.

Have you got yourself into some tight situation you cannot come out of? Do you feel guilty about that? There is no reason for guilt. Repent for that act and ask for forgiveness. But be sure that even in that case God is right there with you. In many situations, we fail to see how God prospers us even in the storm. This is because instead of lifting our eyes up to Him, we tend to look down and pay attention to the problem instead of the deliverer. So we put on an ungrateful attitude towards God and allow ourselves to be overcome by our problems. Listen to what God says, *"He will call upon me, and I will answer him; I will be with him in trouble, I will deliver him and honor him"* (Psalm 91:15).

His ever-true promise is that He will be with you in trouble just as He was with Joseph. God never abandons His own. No matter the problem you have, God is there with you. He will be with you in trouble, not some but all your troubles. What a blessing it will be if only you take your eyes off the troublesome circumstances in which you find yourself and look up to God who is right there with you. As you look up to Him, the brilliance of His face will penetrate you and bring healing to your inmost being and soon, you will find that though the trouble is still there, though it may even intensify, your heart will be full of joy and gratitude.

God has not only promised to be with you in trials but also to deliver you from them. He has His timing for everything; do not think He will forget you. He has promised to deliver, His words are true. In due time He will deliver. This calls for patience, perseverance, and endurance on your part. Look forth with patience and expectation to the day of your deliverance. He says after deliverance, He will honor you. More on that later!

Always, storms and flames in life are schools in which our Heavenly Father who knows what is good for us enrolls us so that we may learn vital and indispensable lessons. Joseph who had to become Prime Minister of Egypt had to learn how to manage a household. One who was sold as a slave soon had charge of all that Potiphar owned. Through him, God blessed Potiphar's household and business. God may well take us through storms so that through us, He might bless others and prove His goodness and kindness to a world which will otherwise keep Him out, a world which knows nothing of Him. He wants to use us to reach out to the world that knows nothing of His unfailing love, His mercy and compassion, His grace that increases infinitely in time of need. This may well require that He takes us through storms. Glory to His holy Name!

Chapter Three

Trials in the Storm

"Now Joseph was well-built and handsome, and after a while his master's wife took notice of Joseph and said, 'Come to bed with me!' But he refused. 'With me in charge,' he told her, 'my master does not concern himself with anything in the house; everything he owns he has entrusted to my care. No one is greater in this house than I am. My master has withheld nothing from me except you, because you are his wife. How then could I do such a wicked thing and sin against God?' And though she spoke to Joseph day after day, he refused to go to bed with her or even be with her. One day he went into the house to attend to his duties, and none of the household servants was inside. She caught him by his cloak and said, 'Come to bed with me!' But he left his cloak in her hand and ran out of the house. When she saw that he had left his cloak in her hand and had run out of the house, she called her household servants. 'Look,' she said to them, 'this Hebrew has been brought to us to make sport of us! He came in here to sleep with me, but I screamed. When he heard me scream for help, he left his cloak beside me and ran out of the house.' She kept his cloak beside her until his master came home. Then she told him this story: 'That Hebrew slave you brought us came to me to make sport of me. But as soon as I screamed for help, he left his cloak beside me and ran out of the house.' When his master heard the story his wife told him, saying, 'This is how your slave treated me,' he burned with anger. Joseph's master took him

and put him in prison, the place where the king's prisoners were confined" (Genesis 39:6b-20a).

Many trials will come your way when you are going through storms. At such times, you need more than ever to implore God's grace and strength to walk in white and uprightness. You will have many sinful offers. Sin will become cheap to commit. Satan's agents will make promises to you; promises to free you from the storms if you take sides with Satan, promises of a better future if only you compromise just a little.

Here, Joseph was tempted to accept *"free sex"* and be in good terms with his mistress or refuse and be set up. I strongly believe Joseph knew the aftermath of his decision not to compromise. He however refused to sin against God and against his master. Others would have seized the opportunity to possess what their master had, for to gain the wife of a man is to gain all what the man possesses. Not so with Joseph, he feared God. One thing is clear here, unless the fear of God is written on your heart in bold print with the blood of the Lamb, you will find yourself compromising and bringing shame and dishonor to the name of God.

How many employees have compromised with their employers to cheat the government for fear of persecution or dismissal? How many teachers have taken sides with their principals to permit cheating in exams? May God convict you of betraying His honor for some worthless gain! Have you decided *"to gain the whole world and forfeit your own soul"*?

Avoid the Bait

Let me point out something here: Joseph could well have compromised and received the temporary gain, but through this act he would have forfeited his soul and his dream to mount the throne. Joseph knew who he was and where he was heading. He had faith that one day, his dream will be realized. He trusted God for it and so refused to compromise. May I say here that there will be many shortcuts to end life's storms! But never use any shortcut; that will just take you into a bigger unanticipated problem which may lead to the loss of many lives.

Chapter 3: Trials in the Storm 17

Do you remember David and Saul? Though David had two clear opportunities to slay Saul and end his suffering, he did not. He decided to go full scale and allow God to determine his course. Take the Lord Jesus, our supreme example: Satan offered Him the Kingdoms of this world, but He knew what He was up to and could rebuke this tempter. When He hung on that cross, remember what many said to Him; *"if you are the Son of God, come down from that cross and we will believe in you"*. What an opportunity for Jesus to have proven the legitimacy of His claims. It was even advantageous; He could not have gone through the agony of death. But, no! He knew why He came. He knew what He was out for. He accepted to go through all of it. And today we can celebrate His victory over death, we can sing of the victory on that Easter morning.

My dear friend, always ask for grace to get through the storm and to shun all shortcuts. Every child of God needs to know who he or she is in Christ; his inheritance, rights, and privileges. And even in the most trying circumstances you shall shun all the offers of the world and Satan, and hold on to the promises of God.

When hope fades into oblivion

So we see Joseph who had just begun enjoying a bit of relief and prosperity faced with another storm. Now he had to lose his freedom and became a prisoner because of his righteousness. Oh! That each one of God's children may know that this world has nothing good for anyone who holds on to the standards of God. All will seem to be against you in this generation of crooks and perverts. They shall try in every way to destroy you and destroy your faith. Do not mind, God is there with you. We have no record of how Joseph tried to justify himself, he accepted it. For he knew God holds the future. Permit me ask you a question; how do you react to problems? What is your attitude to those who slander you, those who set you up? How I find myself wanting! God, have mercy!

Many a time, you think your deliverance or salvation has come, only to realize your world begins to crumble again. The little hope built begins to fade and the future seems to hold nothing but gloom and despair. Life seems to bring endless suffering and pain. We lose that which we acquired and again we are overcome by despair. This was not so with Joseph, he had confidence in God. His confidence was steadfastly anchored on to God through his dreams and held unswervingly to that which he had proclaimed. Oh Lord, fill our hearts with faith in you, may the hope we have be truly an anchor to our souls, and may we trust and believe You at all times, in all places, whether in pains, in sorrow, in need, or in sickness.

God's Unending Favor

> *"Joseph's master took him and put him in prison, the place where the king's prisoners were confined. But while Joseph was there in the prison, the LORD was with him; he showed him kindness and granted him favor in the eyes of the prison warden. So the warden put Joseph in charge of all those held in the prison, and he was made responsible for all that was done there. The warden paid no attention to anything under Joseph's care, because the LORD was with Joseph and gave him success in whatever he did"* (Genesis 39:20-23).

I am amazed at how far, the world may go to slander God's children who refuse to dance to their tune. They spare no effort to make sure you suffer the consequences of crimes you never committed. Oh! That you and I leave no trace through which the world may accuse us. If they do, it should be false accusations. Give them no reason to persecute you except that you would not dance to their tune, that you would not sing their song. Though they may try to intimidate you with false evidence, do not give in to them, stand your ground on the Rock that abides forever.

Have you realized that often in cases where the righteous are involved, the presiding judge gives them no opportunity to explain? All charges against them are always true. Do not worry; our home is somewhere else, where they cannot go. We live as strangers in their world but in ours, there are no strangers, only citizens. Take a look once more at verse 21. God will show you His unlimited favor as long as you uphold the standards. No matter how many times the storms *"pull you down"* God will raise you up, prosper you and restore that which the storm took away, sixty or hundred folds.

Chapter 3: Trials in the Storm

Here in prison, Joseph had to learn how to manage a different set of people. This time they were not servants who were free and paid but prisoners. They had lost their freedom and were confined in small cells, separated from love ones. In this prison, you could find those who earned their prison terms while others were put there unjustly like himself. I believe this is the most trying responsibility; to manage crooks, some hardened, and others hopeless. In prison, Joseph had to learn to share the pain of those who are treated unjustly. He had to learn to uplift the souls of the downcast and minister to the oppressed.

One thing is sure, in all these, Joseph was growing in the school of administration, both public and private. Let us look at some of the specialties he had validated:

1. The specialty of shepherd supervision
2. The specialty of household slavery.
3. The specialty of household management.
4. The specialty of business management.
5. The specialty of penitentiary administration.

God wants His children to work, He wants them to learn to do small things, and He will prosper them even in the most despised vocations. If you hold onto God and not give in to circumstances, His unending favors will always be yours in times of need.

His Attitude in the Storm

I recommend that you read through Genesis forty to better understand what will be said here. Before you continue, quickly read through that chapter. Almost all that will be said here will be based on this.

God always allows things to come our way according to His eternal plan and infinite knowledge. What happens to us affects people positively if we stay cool and trust and believe Him. More often than not, the storms we face may save a whole family, village, tribe, city, nation etc. Our responses to God in the storm will determine how far God will go in working out His purposes in the lives of others. Since none of us lives as an island, what happens to you will affect the life of others positively or negatively.

There are storms, which will carry you away from home, away from loved ones, protection and property, so where you are taken to you can become God's missionary. According to God's plan for Joseph, the prison was to be the gateway to honor and glory. What happened to him in prison determined the course of the rest of his life on this planet. The course of a considerable period in your life is determined by what happens to you in the situation you find yourself in. No storm ends in itself. Its merits or demerits follow us far longer than we can ever know, maybe far down to our third generation.

In prison, Joseph had to exercise his spiritual gift of interpretation and administration diligently. Most often, many people allow themselves to be battered by problems. Are you such? You have allowed problems to weigh you down until you now find yourself unable to use your spiritual gifts. Have you allowed them to be buried in the storm? Have you failed to render the ministry God expects you to render? Where you are, in that situation, have you failed to reveal God to your environment?

The sad thing is that many people's attitudes in the storm will give little or no opportunity for the exercise of spiritual gifts. How can you use the gifts to bless others when you are filled with self-pity and all what you see is yourself. Though thousands whose problems are more serious than yours come near you, you fail to see them because your own problem has been magnified to an extent which only God knows.

Many tend to magnify their problems far beyond that of any other person such that even though there are multitudes of needy, oppressed, lonely, frustrated, discouraged people around, they see only themselves and their own problems. Have you, due to self-love, refused to see what God is showing you concerning the needs of others? Have you refused to hear the cry of the oppressed? Do you think your problem is final?

Your attitude in the storm may lead the world to see that you have something, a secret strength that they do not have or that Christianity is a miserable course. Had Joseph been caught up with himself and failed to interpret the dreams, it is obvious that he could have stayed much longer in prison. Will it be wrong if one attributes the delay in your deliverance from the storm to the fact that you have been too caught up with yourself? All you have seen up to now is your own problem; all you long for is your own deliverance. Don't you think that if you begin to concern yourself with providing solutions to the problems of others your deliverance will come?

Have you through self-centeredness been blocking your own deliverance? Get out of your cocoon, get out of your personal kingdom and reach out to others and before long a song of praise will flow from your lips to the God of heaven. May be I say it again in other words; many of us stay longer than we were supposed to in the storms of life because we fail to accomplish the purpose for which God allowed it to come our way.

The consequences would have been great had Joseph failed to interpret the dreams. Multitudes would have perished, his entire family would have starved to death in the future, and Egypt would have been wiped out along with the nations around. Does that give you a picture of how your attitude in a storm can influence a very large sphere of people you know nothing about? May you be prepared in season and out of season to put to use that which God has invested in you, to make the most of every opportunity when the need arises, no matter the storm beating around you!

You can be of help to at least one person. I say this as seen in this passage and from my personal experience. In times when I have forgotten about my own problems reached out to others, I have realized that my deliverance has come suddenly, my needs have been met and the lives of others have been blessed. On the other hand, when I have carried on me my problems, my facial expression alone has scared those around and I have just been alone in *"my world"* unconcerned about others. God, have mercy on me! The truth is that, blame no one for your lack of deliverance, for you hold the key to that closed door. When Joseph exercised his spiritual gift he went on to pour out his heart to the one to whom he had shown kindness. He then asked for a favor from this guy. Maybe the reason for which you have not found anyone to share your problem with is because you still see no one whose condition is worse than yours.

Misplaced Expectation!

> *"But when all goes well with you, remember me and show me kindness; mention me to Pharaoh and get me out of this prison. For I was forcibly carried off from the land of the Hebrews, and even here I have done nothing to deserve being put in a dungeon"* (Genesis 40:14-15).

At this point in time we see Joseph moving his attention from God to man. What longing, what expectation for deliverance! But only it was wrongly placed. Do you see his words in verse 15? These words are true, but in them are expressions of disappointment and complain. Joseph who has acted *"supernaturally"* all along returned to the natural plain as soon as he turned his attention from God to man.

The source of strength and peace in times of storms is God alone. Once you move your attention from Him, your faith begins to crumble and you start grumbling and complaining and might end up in a depression. Though each of us may reach this point, it must not be so. As soon as you realize that you have shifted your attention from God to something else, repent and ask for grace to keep on hoping for His deliverance when it shall come, not if it shall come.

It is not surprising that the cup-bearer forgot Joseph in prison. Those who place their trust in man will often than not be disappointed. In most cases, those we help in their hour of need seem to forget us when we need them in our own trials. They fail to render us the ministry we might well benefit from. This shows that your deliverance can never originate from man. Man can never work it out, no matter how you try, no matter how much you mediate. Until God's appointed time reaches, there will be no hope on the horizon. Learn to persevere and wait on God for your deliverance. *"Though it lingers, wait for it, it will certainly come and will not delay"* (Habakkuk 2:3b).

Evaluate Yourself

Is your hope for deliverance from your current storm in God or in some organization, somebody, or something? Are you trying to mediate your own deliverance? Are you asking someone to see somebody for you? <u>Be sure that until God intervenes, any deliverance anyone tries to bring, though it may seem real, will end up being a farce and plunge you into a deeper level of despair, gloom, pain, and sorrow</u>. God in His mercy may cause that one in whom you place the hope for deliverance to forget you.

Though God may use institutions, people, or things to bring us deliverance, our hope must not and should not be placed on them but on Him and on Him alone. I believe after having waited for the expected deliverance to no avail, Joseph once again came to his right mind and placed his confidence where it belonged, in God. As soon as he did this, heaven began working out his deliverance.

Chapter Four

Through the Storm to Glory

From the time Joseph left his father's house in search of his brothers, it was one problem after another. He got lost in the desert unable to trace his brothers. He narrowly escaped death in the hands of his own brothers, was thrown into a cistern without water, was later sold as a slave and now ended up in jail. From any human point of view, there was no hope for Joseph. All what could be anticipated for him was suffering, endless suffering. Even those who sold him into slavery did so in order that they may *"see what becomes of his dreams"*. Their goal was to destroy the vision and the vision only. But in ignorance they were executing God's will for Joseph.

Sometimes, those who appear as our enemies, though they intend to harm us, God turns it out to accomplish His will for us, and even for a whole generation, race, nation, or continent. May we learn to see God in everything good or bad! As long as you are right with God, through Him, see everything that comes your way. See Him in the arrows which pierce your heart. See Him in the disappointments. See Him in all things, and see all things through His own eyes. Has He not promised to be a *"wall of fire around you"*? Thus anything which reaches you passes first through the wall of fire. The fire burns away the harmful components; it tests and purifies everything which touches your life.

As Joseph waited in jail, he began trusting God once more; God began working out His deliverance. Though the cup-bearer had forgotten Joseph, it was time for God to remind him of his short-comings. At God's time, Joseph was mentioned to Pharaoh, not on the basis of having been 'forcibly carried off from the land of the Hebrews, and even here I have done nothing to deserve being put in a dungeon' but on the basis of having played his God-ordained role of interpreting the dreams of the servants of Pharaoh. He had used his gifts to serve servants and now was an opportunity to serve the highest authority in Egypt.

Your gift is your open door

Do you desire to use your spiritual gifts to serve only the high class or only the great? Is that the reason why until now you've had no opportunity to exercise your gifts and year after year they are dwindling? Before God gives you promotion to serve the great, you have to begin serving the small, the very scum of the earth. Without this I promise you that you have no hope. Until you're contented with small beginnings there's no great future for one who must be extensively used by God. Joseph started his ministry in the prison cell, serving prisoners, rendering ministry to those who had lost their freedom and so God could give him the promotion which he had.

What relief Joseph had when he received word that Pharaoh wanted him! His old friend had told Pharaoh about him, Pharaoh sent for him immediately, and he was quickly brought from the dungeon. Man, when God brings deliverance, it is swift and effective. No half measures. 'Though it lingers wait for it, it will not delay'. It is never a slow process; He starts and brings it to completion at once. That is the nature of His working. We do not know for how long Joseph stayed in prison without a haircut or a change of clothes. But as soon as his deliverance came, we could see the changes it brought. The old clothes had to go. The shabby look had to disappear. When God brings deliverance, the evidences are glaring and never hidden. People will see your change of character, the old garment of sin and worldliness will be changed and the garment of Christ-likeness put on. God's deliverance brings along benefits and not trouble.

Take no glory for yourself

Now here is Joseph before Pharaoh, who put all his hope in him for interpretation. Though Joseph knew past successes in the exercise of his gifts and ministry, at least the ones in the prison, he had no confidence in himself. He never placed any confidence in the flesh or in experience. He never claimed he could interpret dreams. He depended on God alone so he could say *"I cannot do it" but God would give Pharaoh the answer he desires"* (Genesis 41:16). This is true humility. May you and I like Joseph, learn to give God all the glory due Him without any attempt or secret desire to share it.

When God begins to use you in an extensive way, the tendency is to have a growing confidence in yourself and in experience. You must guard against it. Though you must be confident, your confidence should lie on nothing else but on the power of God, the victory of Christ Jesus on the cross of Calvary, which by the new birth became yours. God gave Joseph the interpretation of the dreams and wisdom on how to manage the situation. Some would have told Pharaoh, *"God has told me how this must be handled, if you make me Prime Minister, I will help manage the situation and spare you and your people from the effects of this famine"*.

Some would have labored to use the gifts of God for selfish ends. How many people are using their gifts to find their way to higher positions in Christian circles? How many are using their gifts and Ministry to amass wealth from helpless people in need? How many have used their gift to draw attention to themselves and caused many to depend on them, instead of God? They make sure without them nothing happens so indeed they can be celebrated as indispensable. May God expose the corruption of such hearts! Joseph sought no selfish interest. He did not keep the God-revealed plan to himself but was willing to make it known to Pharaoh. He gave every detail of it to the governing council of Egypt.

Unlike Joseph, in our desperation, we labor to gain man's recognition and so we are committed to do anything to gain favor from man even at the cost of our spirituality. Let us cease to portray ourselves and labor to be filled with the

Spirit of God. When men realize we have the Spirit of God in us, we will be duly honored; we do not have to prove our worth. Truly, in this world, the question can always be asked *"can we find any one like this man, one in whom is the Spirit of God"*? (Genesis 41:38). <u>The greatest need of the Church and the world today is for Spirit-filled, anointed men and women to occupy positions of influence and leadership. Men who are willing to use the wisdom of God for the welfare of everybody and not as a means for selfish gain! Nobody, no matter how educated or influential or rich equals the task of a Spirit-filled man or woman.</u>

Reward for Self-effacement

> *"Then Pharaoh said to Joseph, 'Since God has made all this known to you, there is no one so discerning and wise as you. You shall be in charge of my palace, and all my people are to submit to your orders. Only with respect to the throne will I be greater than you.' So Pharaoh said to Joseph, ' hereby put you in charge of the whole land of Egypt.' Then Pharaoh took his signet ring from his finger and put it on Joseph's finger. He dressed him in robes of fine linen and put a gold chain around his neck. He had him ride in a chariot as his second-in-command, and men shouted before him, 'Make way!' Thus he put him in charge of the whole land of Egypt. Then Pharaoh said to Joseph, 'I am Pharaoh, but without your word no one will lift hand or foot in all Egypt.' Pharaoh gave Joseph the name Zaphenath-Paneah and gave him Asenath daughter of Potiphera, priest of On, to be his wife. And Joseph went throughout the land of Egypt"* (Genesis 41:39-45).

Let us outline the glories into which Joseph walked from a prison cell. Pharaoh said;

1. You shall be in charge of my palace.
2. All my people are to submit to your orders.
3. Only with respect to the throne will I be greater than you.
4. I hereby put you in charge of the whole land of Egypt.

Pharaoh did the following to him:
1. Put his signet ring on Joseph's finger.
2. Dressed him in robes of fine linen.
3. Put a gold chain around his neck.
4. Had him ride in a chariot as second in command.
5. Escorts went before Joseph
6. Made him a co-signatory to every order or decree.
7. Gave him a new name.
8. Gave him a wife.

I had never understood the details like this before. By the time I started listing them I was amazed that the list just continued. How good, how lovely, how generous is your God! When He blesses, He does so exceedingly more than what we can ever expect. Do you see now why Joseph had to go through several schools of management and administration? May we be patient enough to learn our lessons in the schools into which our Heavenly Father enrolls us!

The Pathway to Glory

> *"Before the years of famine came, two sons were born to Joseph by Asenath daughter of Potiphera, priest of On. Joseph named his firstborn Manasseh and said, "It is because God has made me forget all my trouble and all my father's household." The second son he named Ephraim and said, "It is because God has made me fruitful in the land of my suffering"*
> (Genesis 41:50-52).

When God takes you through troubles, He makes you forget them. The former things are forgotten because the glory at the end of every storm far surpasses the pain incurred. God will make you forget the wrong that people ever did to you and cause you to see His goodness in the glories enjoyed after patiently enduring the storm. That was the first lesson Joseph drew from his experience after the storm, so he named his first son Manasseh.

He named his second son Ephraim and said *"It is because God has made me fruitful in the land of my suffering"*. That was the second lesson he drew out of it. Oh! How many think God allows suffering in order to destroy them and so render themselves fruitless and useless. No! God wants to make you fruitful and useful even in the land of your suffering, no matter what it may be, no matter how impossible it may appear. God wants to make you fruitful, even in that strange land, among strange people.

Do you really want to be fruitful in the land of your suffering? Then cooperate with God so you can first of all forget all your troubles. Until you forgive and forget the sins of those whom God used to bring about your suffering, do not expect to be fruitful. As long as you hold anything against anybody at any time, forget fruitfulness. It is first of all forgetting then becoming fruitful, that is the order.

The God Who Restores

Here is Joseph, a man once confined in a prison cell, now travelling all over Egypt. A man who was stripped of his richly ornamented robe now wearing robes of linen! A man accused of attempted rape, now given a wife of his own, and many more honors. Through the storms, Joseph became the vessel of honor in Egypt and beyond.

Chapter Five

A Persistent Storm

Remember we earlier mentioned Jacob and promised to return to him later. As we said, Jacob was still proving too strong and stubborn to learn the lesson in the school in which God had enrolled him. He always found a new object on which to place his love and affection apart from God Himself. After Rachael's death, Joseph became the new object of his love and now Joseph had mysteriously disappeared. After Joseph's apparent death, his father transferred his love to Benjamin.

Benjamin became the new object of his love, the new *"Idol"* in his heart. The new thing he could offer his all to protect-that which he labored to keep from harm. By inheriting the love due his mother and brother, Benjamin became the center of his father's concern. Now, there was famine in the land and there was an urgent need for corn. There was a need for corn, someone had to go in search for corn in Egypt and so he decided to send his sons except Benjamin. He wanted to live and not die but he would not send the idol of his heart. All else could go, but not this dear idol, not this god, for no harm should come to it.

Wait a minute! Before you condemn Jacob, let me ask you some personal questions and may God speak to your heart so that in all honesty you may respond to the prompting of His Spirit with respect to exposing the idols in your own very life. What is that thing you have labored to protect all these years at the cost of every other thing? What is that object that takes your love supremely apart from the Savior? For Jacob it was Benjamin.

> *"Then ten of Joseph's brothers went down to buy grain from Egypt. But Jacob did not send Benjamin, Joseph's brother, with the others, because he was afraid that harm might come to him"* (Genesis 42:3-4).

The ten brothers could go and harm could come to them, no problem. But Benjamin, no way! No harm should come to him. For if harm came to him, it came to his father also. At this point in time, Israel thought he had succeeded to guard his idol. Until now no harm had come and so his trust, love, commitment, and devotion to this idol increased. More loyalty, more allegiance to this new god of his heart! I counsel you to read the rest of the story.

There came a moment when God had to strike hard. At this time I believe Jacob would learn his final lesson to enthrone God and Him alone on his heart, to put Him where He rightly belongs but only after having suffered much. He arrived a point where he had no other option. God placed him in a tight corner. There was now just one way out, the overthrow of the idol of his heart. Listen to what he said.

> *"Their father Jacob said to them, "You have deprived me of my children. Joseph is no more and Simeon is no more, and now you want to take Benjamin. Everything is against me!"* (Genesis 42:36)

Do you Feel like the whole World is against you?

Has there been a time in your life when you felt everything was against you? Moments when you felt even God had risen against you? Many times when we are in trouble, due to our wrong attitudes, we think our loving Father now hates us; we think the one who seeks our good now seeks our downfall; we think the One who is our shield has now become a sword against us; we think our Guide has turned His back on us. But No! He still loves and cares.

Chapter 5: A Persistent Storm

Often, at such moments, we lose confidence in almost everybody around us and probably begin to find faults in those who serve us in one way or another.

Though Jacob was in a tight corner, he would not let go of Benjamin. He was hungry, the whole family was starving but he cared less if all died, only that Benjamin be protected. Jacob refused to trust anyone, he could entrust Benjamin to no one's care, for this god was his and not that of the family. In spite of all the effects nothing could change his position.

> "But Jacob said, 'My son will not go down there with you; his brother is dead and he is the only one left. If harm comes to him on the journey you are taking, you will bring my gray head down to the grave in sorrow'" (Genesis 42:38).

Touch the idol of a man and his whole world comes crumbling, for to it is attached his mind, will, and emotions; and sorrow will be his portion for the rest of his life if Christ is not enthroned. Jacob blamed his sons for his misfortune and saw everything wrong in everyone but his idol. But God had not relented, the famine was intensifying and he had to just do something. Though he blamed others, that did not help one little bit. In your current situation, don't see anything wrong with anybody; see no one as the cause of your misfortune but as a tool in God's hands, to break your pride, to overthrow that idol on God's throne, and to purge the temple of all the impurities.

Did Jacob really give in? Not quite, someone had to guarantee something. At first, Reuben did and his was rejected, why? Firstly, he had forfeited his right as the first born by defiling his father's bed. Do you know you can forfeit your right to the Spirit's anointing? Your rights to the authority of the cross can be forfeited due to sin and idolatry? That God may speak to your heart!

Secondly, because he did not put himself or his own life at stake, all what he could guarantee were his sons, innocent children. Are you a parent? Are the lives of your children precious to you? Can you lay down your life for them? It is a sad thing to know that some parents sell their children for money. They sell them to Satan only if in return they can make a profit. Parents, does the spiritual life of your child matter to you? Or do you prefer that he or she dies spiritually to obtain a vocation, spouse or whatever? That God would convict you and expose your secret longings, wishes and desires for the children He has entrusted you with. Third reason why Reuben's offer was rejected is because Reuben symbolizes human strength which is a hindrance to the working of the Holy Spirit.

Let Praise Take the Lead

After the storm became severe, Judah (Praise) came forth, guaranteeing the boy's safety with his own life, not with anything else but with his own life. Do you see that their salvation now depended on Judah? Much of what you and I can ever receive depends on the praise we offer. Praises not only in times of joy, but praises which are sacrifices. If you praise God in whatever you do, then your confidence in Him will grow, even your storms and the days of famine will quickly be shortened.

Verse 10 of chapter 43 lets us know that, as long as praise is delayed from our lips the longer our deliverance takes to come. <u>When praise comes to the scene we can reap twice the benefits of the storm</u>. When praise came in, Jacob gave in. He said, *"Take your brother also and go back to the man at once. And may God Almighty grant you mercy before the man so that he will let your other brother and Benjamin come back with you. As for me, if I am bereaved, I am bereaved"* (Genesis 43:13-14).

Now Jacob was prepared for anything. He let go his idol, and as soon as he let go this idol, God took his rightful place. Jacob once again came to put his trust in God and in Him alone. He saw in a new way that all depended on EL-Shaddai – God Almighty. Do you see what attachment to things and to people can cause you? You will be totally blind to the greatness of God and to what He can do in your life. <u>Maybe the reason why God is not so real to you is because of your attachment to other things enthroned on your heart</u>. Overthrow those idols and let God be enthroned, let Christ take His place in your life as Lord and King.

<u>We always try to protect that which is dear to us and hold on to it. We would not allow God to be our protector but the storm will persistently become severe</u>

until we let go and rely on God. God does not give up on His own, neither does He give in to them.

The Dream Comes True

In a new way, this account of Joseph is increasingly becoming interesting to me. I discover each time, new truths and practicalities which will carry me onto a different plane in my walk with God. If you carefully read through this narrative, God will show you deep truths, which will illuminate your soul. The rest of the story is told in Genesis 44 – 50.

It had taken Joseph more than twenty years to realize his dreams; thirteen years before coming into Pharaoh's service and seven years of abundance preparing for the famine. Then his brothers came and bowed down to the ground in honor to him.

> "Now Joseph was the governor of the land, the one who sold grain to all its people. So when Joseph's brothers arrived, they bowed down to him with their faces to the ground" (Genesis 42:6).

In spite of all the tides, in spite of the persistent storm, in spite of all the attempts to destroy his vision, this dream came true at last. He stayed in God's shelter and realized his dreams. If your dream has God at the origin, if your dream is rooted in nothing else but Christ, then no matter the opposition you are facing now, no matter the threat, as you trust in God, your dreams will come true. You will not need to fight anybody, you will not need to defend or justify yourself, and you will not need to avenge anything. You simply need to trust the One who gave you the dream. You just need to stay cool and relax in Him as your refuge – your shelter in the time of storm.

Do you have a dream? It might not come to accomplishment too soon as you thought or think; it may take longer than you think. But if you endure the storms which come to prepare you for the dream, in due time you will be there.

Those who try to destroy the vision or dreams of others will themselves know no peace. This sin they commit shall haunt them all the days of their life. There is no peace for the wicked; your sin will always find you out. Maybe you think you can go away with it. Never! It may take time; ten, twenty, or even fifty years to hide your sin but you shall be brought to light and exposed. No one sins against man and against God and goes away with it. You had better come out of your hiding place and repent of that sin, of that conspiracy against that man of God, against that bearer of the vision before it becomes too late.

Do you encourage the young people in the Ministry or you labor to throw cold water on them, such that their vision instead of burning is placed on ice? It is very shocking that there are some old "believers" in some assemblies who are not going anywhere. They have been there for long without any vision or purpose and will do everything in criticism and cynicism to ensure that the young believers go nowhere. In their rebellion against authority they seek to gather people who do not know where they are going and together rise up against bearers of God's vision, against those aflame for God. And they are going to end at nothing but at putting out the flame. May God truly be the shelter of His vision bearers!

Beyond Expectations!

When Jacob received the news that Joseph was still alive, he could not believe it at first. However he was persuaded and so he decided to go see things for himself.

> *"So Israel set out with all that was his, and when he reached Beersheba, he offered sacrifices to the God of his father Isaac. And God spoke to Israel in a vision at night and said, 'Jacob! Jacob!' 'Here I am,' he replied. 'I am God, the God of your father,' he said. 'Do not be afraid to go down to Egypt, for I will make you into a great nation there. ^{4} I will go down to Egypt with you, and I will surely bring you back again. And Joseph's own hand will close your eyes'"* (Genesis 46:1-4).

Oh! How much storms can steal from us! Throughout this time, Jacob had offered no sacrifice to God. He was caught up with his problems. He had decided to stay in sorrow and in mourning for the rest of his life. His spirit was now dead, no sensitivity to God, no sensitivity to the interests and needs of God. The channel of communion between him and God was broken, because he allowed the problem he faced to crush him down and deprive him of this singular honor and privilege of communion with God. My dear friend, though you and I are weak, we have a God on whose strength to stand on, whose grace we can implore, whose hand we can hold on, whose love we can trust. May we explore our privileges to the fullest!

Have you been battered in the storm? Ask God to revive your spirit so once more you can look up to Him. The Bible says, when Jacob heard and saw signs, his spirit revived (Genesis 45:27). When his spirit was revived, he set out in faith and *"he offered sacrifices to the God of his father Isaac"*. When revival comes into a man's life, his first response is a faith venture. The altar of sacrifice and communion is immediately restored.

Have you pulled down the altar of communion and sacrifice in your life due to the storms? Is that why Heaven has been silent for this long? God wants to speak, but your spirit is dead, the altar of sacrifice and communion is in ruins. Often than not, the reason why Heaven always seems so silent is because we would not give it a chance to speak to us. If you repair the altar of praise and sacrifice in your life, you will begin to hear the voice of your Father: His voice of assurance, His voice of comfort, His voice of revelation of things to come, His voice of confirmation and of direction.

The surprise

> *"Israel said to Joseph, "I never expected to see your face again, and now God has allowed me to see your children too"* (Genesis 48:11).

Our God is a God of surprises and of restoration. That which is momentarily taken from us during the storm, in due time, will be restored in an exceeding measure. Joseph was taken away from Jacob, so he could enthrone God in his heart. After he learnt this lesson, through many failures, Joseph was restored to him, not alone but with two other sons. One became three! If you persevere and go through the storms you are facing, God will restore to you double and even triple of all that you lost as a result of the storm. On the other side of the storm, lies surprises for you, thrilling days of celebration and jubilation. For some, it will be in this life, for others in the life to come. <u>When we finally give up our struggle to keep what we cannot keep, God guards for us and gives it to us in due time with an extra bonus.</u>

Do you have a dream? Hold onto it, though the way to achieving it may be narrow and rocky and stormy, hold onto God and persist and endure. When you go through, you are not going to regret it in anyway. You shall forever be joyful that you went through and that the storms came your way. Praise the Lord! Glory to His Name!

Part Two

The Life of Job

We just saw the life of Joseph, a young man with dreams and aspirations who went through the storms on to glory and honour. In spite of all the storms, he succeeded in attaining his dreams. Not everybody who is going through storms falls in this category. In this section, we are going to see the life of Job, a man who had attained his dreams and wishes and was living in security, luxury, and comfort. He feared God. In this category, some will quickly identify themselves. The problems in which they now find themselves are similar to those of Job. Like the previous case, God has something to say to those concerned.

As we go through the story of Job, allow God to speak to your heart. May you be open to receive the ministry He has in store for you and in all sincerity, may you respond to His voice, be it of comfort, correction, or rebuke. May you draw from it inspiration to push ahead where necessary, to stay put when required, and always to trust and hope in the Lord your God, or more intimately your Father, loving Father; all powerful, all knowing. He is always available. This is the foundation of your hope in times of trials, and of our hope beyond the storms of life. How I long that our Heavenly Father may speak His words of life to us afresh as we go through these pages and where dry bones are, may they rise to life once more to the glory of His Name.

Chapter Six

Successful and Secure

"In the land of Uz there lived a man whose name was Job. This man was blameless and upright; he feared God and shunned evil. He had seven sons and three daughters, and he owned seven thousand sheep, three thousand camels, five hundred yoke of oxen and five hundred donkeys, and had a large number of servants. He was the greatest man among all the people of the East. His sons used to take turns holding feasts in their homes, and they would invite their three sisters to eat and drink with them. When a period of feasting had run its course, Job would send and have them purified. Early in the morning he would sacrifice a burnt offering for each of them, thinking, "Perhaps my children have sinned and cursed God in their hearts." This was Job's regular custom" (Job. 1:1-5).

We live today in a generation where the majority is craving for more wealth, comfort, and luxury. People work day and night tirelessly to obtain wealth. Some will stop at nothing to satisfy their greed, even to the extent of taking away the life of innocent souls. The average man craves for more of this, more of that, more here, more there, more of everything everywhere. Many have laid on the altar of materialism the rare jewel of contentment which they once possessed. Communion with God has been viewed as an obstacle and now lies in the ruins. Such wealth when obtained acts as security and those who possess it feel protected and secured, though inwardly, there is a sense of insecurity, fear of death, of thieves etc.

Job was a healthy and extremely wealthy man, blameless and upright both in the sight of God and of man. He feared God and shunned evil. This is a very challenging description. In our world today, even in Christian circles, it is rare to find men of enormous wealth who stand upright and blameless. The acquisition of wealth for many can be attributed to diverse ways of crockery and manipulation of others. They do everything to obtain profit even if it means depriving others of their basic rights.

James cried out against these rich people when he said:

> *"Now listen, you rich people, weep and wail because of the misery that is coming upon you. Your wealth has rotted, and moths have eaten your clothes. Your gold and silver are corroded. Their corrosion will testify against you and eat your flesh like fire. You have hoarded wealth in the last days. Look! The wages you failed to pay the workmen who mowed your fields are crying out against you. The cries of the harvesters have reached the ears of the Lord Almighty. You have lived on earth in luxury and self-indulgence. You have fattened yourselves in the day of slaughter. You have condemned and murdered innocent men, who were not opposing you"* (James 5:1-6).

See how many are hoarding wealth in these last days, even professing Christians are not left out. Do you pay your workers the wages due them? Those who labor for you, do you satisfy them? If God were to describe you, what will He say concerning your wealth? The things you are amassing are the same things which will testify against you on the day of reckoning. Those you are oppressing are certainly crying and their voices are being heard against you. Again, the Spirit of God cries out against such people through Habakkuk.

> *"Woe to him who builds his realm by unjust gain to set his nest on high, to escape the clutches of ruin! You have plotted the ruin of many peoples, shaming your own house and forfeiting your life. The stones of the wall will cry out, and the beams of the woodwork will echo it. Woe to him who builds a city with bloodshed and*

establishes a town by crime! Has not the LORD Almighty determined that the people's labor is only fuel for the fire, that the nations exhaust themselves for nothing?"* (Habakkuk 2:9-13). Does that describe you?

I think I should not dare to mention the fear of God. Today the wealthy are the promoters of evil, no trace of the fear of God in their lives. In the Christian circle, some have grown rich by hoarding that which God expected them to distribute to the poor and needy all around them. Not so with Job. Have you found a man who thinks he is too rich to believe in God, tell him about Job, one who was the greatest amongst the people of the east, the wealthiest, yet had a deep sense of the fear of the Lord in him?

Give some people a quarter of Job's wealth and they will fly crazy. Things will begin to fall apart. God's grace will be trampled underfoot and sensual indulgence will be the order of that life. Job in spite of all his wealth and greatness maintained his integrity in the sight of God and man. He remained a happy man who carried out his responsibility as the priest of the home. It is a tragedy that most wealthy believers allow their children to grow without a true knowledge of God. The parents have failed to teach their children the ways of God because they are carried away by the pressure of business pursuits and gain such that home responsibilities have been greatly or completely abandoned. They lavish their children with wealth and everything but the fear of God.

Children from such homes grow up with an inner void, with a heap of unconfessed sins. Parents, at the end of each day, do you pray for your children? In the simplest of cases, at the start of a new day, do you gather them around the family altar and teach them confession and repentance? Do you teach them the art of sacrifice? Or to you the altars of burnt offerings no longer exist? In a few words, have you abandoned your priestly responsibility such that in your home there is no priest and now anyone does what he or she desires, in what was intended by God to be a sanctuary?

Another lesson we draw from here is that Job's family was happy. In spite of the extreme wealth they had, they were happy and united. They knew the importance of family re-union and the sharing of a common meal at regular intervals. How many families have been destroyed because of strife and greed? Children fight with one another over material things. Each wants to receive the greatest share and greed prevails.

We see a clear and concise Bible account of Job's sources of income. My brother, can you be bold enough in the presence of God's people to honestly declare the sources of your income? Can you expose every business deal you are involved in? If not, then something is wrong somewhere. May you really allow the Spirit to probe your heart!

A Swift Storm

"Then the LORD said to Satan, 'Have you considered my servant Job? There is no one on earth like him; he is blameless and upright, a man who fears God and shuns evil.' 'Does Job fear God for nothing?' Satan replied. 'Have you not put a hedge around him and his household and everything he has? You have blessed the work of his hands, so that his flocks and herds are spread throughout the land. But stretch out your hand and strike everything he has, and he will surely curse you to your face.' The LORD said to Satan, 'Very well, then, everything he has is in your hands, but on the man himself do not lay a finger.' Then Satan went out from the presence of the LORD. One day when Job's sons and daughters were feasting and drinking wine at the oldest brother's house, a messenger came to Job and said, 'The oxen were plowing and the donkeys were grazing nearby, and the Sabeans attacked and carried them off. They put the servants to the sword, and I am the only one who has escaped to tell you!' While he was still speaking, another messenger came and said, 'The fire of God fell from the sky and burned up the sheep and the servants, and I am the only one who has escaped to tell you!' While he was still speaking, another messenger came and said, 'The Chaldeans formed three raiding parties and swept down on your camels and carried them off. They put the servants to the sword, and I am the only one who has escaped to tell you!' While he was still speaking, yet another messenger came and said, 'Your sons and daughters were feasting and drinking wine at the oldest brother's

> house, when suddenly a mighty wind swept in from the desert and struck the four corners of the house. It collapsed on them and they are dead, and I am the only one who has escaped to tell you!' At this, Job got up and tore his robe and shaved his head. Then he fell to the ground in worship and said: 'Naked I came from my mother's womb, and naked I will depart. The LORD gave and the LORD has taken away; may the name of the LORD be praised.' In all this, Job did not sin by charging God with wrongdoing" (Job 1:8-22).

Can God boast of you as He did of Job? Do you appear in the eyes of God and of the devil as holy, pure, and blameless as you appear before man, or is yours a double life? Can God testify of your blamelessness and uprightness? Can God say that you fear Him and shun evil? Are you known in the enemy's camp as one who carries the seal of God? One whose life is in conformity with Biblical teaching and principles? Maybe God has blessed you with wealth, do you fear God because He is God or because of the wealth. Can it be said of you that you fear God for nothing — no selfish interests, no strings attached?

Once, I was travelling in a bus from one city to another. On our way, at small town, we met a funeral convoy. From the kind of vehicles and the length of the convoy, one could tell that a very important person had died. Since they had to cross from one lane to another, our own bus had to stop. We waited for long until we were fed up and began talking in the vehicle, how funerals nowadays have become *"show off"* ceremonies. So I used that opportunity to bring in the gospel by talking about untimely death.

I remember one lady in about her late fifties said she had come to Jesus for protection and that she does not expect anything to happen to her or her children. I cannot really recall all she said but her statements were full of selfish reasons and so I spoke up. I told her if she would not love and fear God just because He is God and that Christ died on the cross to save her and nothing else, she would be in for a shock. I told her if God should permit the death of one of her loved ones, what would she do? Her world and her faith would come crumbling for it stood on the wrong foundation. When she saw with me, I told her to correct her motives and serve and follow Jesus just because He is Lord and Savior and not for what she can get out of Him.

Satan said to the Lord, *"Have you not put a hedge around him and his household and everything he has?"* This is a comforting statement. Our enemy knows it, though in vain he may try to harm us. He knows nothing reaches us without the Father's permission. God has built a hedge which Satan cannot penetrate round you and everything you own. He does nothing without the Father's permission. The only reason Satan can penetrate God's hedge of protection is when you give him legitimacy through sin and rebellion against God.

May Satan, when allowed to test us, find us brave people. May he find that we fear God and serve Him not because of the protection he offers His own but because we delight in serving Him who holds nothing back from us, whom by every standard or reason deserves our devotion and worship. That even when God takes away His protection, our souls will still sing out to Him, the praises, the honour, the majesty, the glory, the power, and dominion due His Name. Indeed, in the words of our Lord *"Do not be afraid of what you are about to suffer. I tell you, the devil will put some of you in prison to test you, and you will suffer persecution for ten days. Be faithful, even to the point of death, and I will give you the crown of life"* (Revelation 2:10).

Designed to Kill

How swift was the calamity that befell Job. Once Satan was given permission by God, he spared nothing and gave Job no time to recover from one shock before the other. Though God had asked him not to touch Job's life, he still thought he could kill Job by bringing one storm after another so swift and abrupt that Job could die from a heart attack. O! How many lie in the grave prematurely because of their reaction to bad news? How many have fallen dead immediately they heard some kind of unpleasant news. How many suffer from stroke and hypertension. God forgive us. If you were in Job's place, would you still be alive after this series of calamities? May the Spirit of God probe your heart and expose the way you react to problems. Ways neither scientifically nor spiritually good for you.

In his attacks, Satan spares no avenue through which he can reach his prey. In this case, he uses man and nature: the sword, fire and wind. Permit me digress here a little: these same weapons Satan uses against the child of God figuratively represent the mighty weapons of spiritual warfare at his disposal. The sword here signifies the word of God. The word of God in the heart of a believer puts the devil to flight. On the other hand, it can be a weapon in the hand of Satan. Do you remember how he used it to attack our Lord? Do you see how false doctrines are rising on the face of the earth? Most of those who propagate false doctrines from hell once walked in the light, but failed to guard this awesome weapon and Satan used it against them and today, thousands, no, millions are being led astray, down the broad lane to hell.

The fire and the wind, when used in scriptures in most cases refer to the Holy Spirit. The Holy Spirit in the life of a believer in power and authority renders him invincible to sin, the world, the flesh, and Satan. He is the source of power and strength for daily living. When He comes into a life, it is either for blessing or for destruction; His presence has never and can never be neutral. Many in the quest for spiritual power have ended up in the fangs of the great serpent — Satan. They have not loved the truth of God but power and Satan has given them counterfeit power which they use to derail others from godliness. With the Holy Spirit in power and authority in our lives, we can influence both man and nature to favor us, commanding them to work against the purposes of Satan and his agents.

Chapter Seven

The Place of Worship

I can imagine the disappointment that gripped Satan's heart, how his face turned sad as he left that scene in the invisible. He aimed at destroying Job's life indirectly. He also aimed at getting Job rebel against God but to his shock, after all the calamity, *"Job got up and tore his robe and shaved his head. Then he fell to the ground in worship"* (v20).

May the problems which come your way lead you to worship. May your response to difficulties be joyous worship, though in tears, to the Lamb who once was slain but now lives forever! If you put up this attitude, then you shall be a constant source of shock and disappointment to Satan and his host. Now consider the following verse:

> *"When Mary reached the place where Jesus was and saw him, she fell at his feet and said, "Lord, if you had been here, my brother would not have died"* (John 11:32).

In moments of sorrow and pain, when the world expects us to mourn, may we run to the feet of the Lord and Savior and fall prostrate in worship and adoration. When the world expects us to complain and grumble, may we instead sing songs of praise and thanksgiving to Him who lives forever. May I say this, and may the Holy Spirit write it deep down the tablet of your heart, may it be engraved permanently and sealed with the blood of the Lamb: <u>The secret to relief in times of sorrow is to fall at the feet of the Savior and there offer acceptable worship.</u> Worship is a sign of surrender. It is a sign of dependence and trust in God. In times of intense pain and sorrow, the best thing to do is to worship and *"stay with Him"*. May children of God be a challenge to Satan and the world, may we in our actions and response to situations defy the thinking of the ordinary man.

> *Job said, "Naked I came from my mother's womb, and naked I will depart. The LORD gave and the LORD has taken away; may the name of the LORD be praised"* (Job 1:21).

Has it dawned on you that you came into the world naked and that you shall return naked? Does your daily life and attitude towards the things in this world bear testimony to the Job kind of life? Wealthy, yet no trust in your wealth? Do you think you will be buried along with any of your wealth? Do you possess the rare jewel of contentment – holy contentment, not the unholy satisfaction with mediocrity, or do you use your godliness as means for financial gain? May God's Holy Spirit search deep down the heart of His children who are erring and heading towards destruction!

Some have used the ministry as a means of exploiting ignorant and innocent people willing to serve their God. How many a crook under the canopy of *"a man of God"* has blocked the way to the gospel because of quest for gain, how many have sacrificed the power of God on the altar of the god of mammon? O! Father cleanse your church, arise and purge the body of your dear Son of such individuals, arise O Lord and sanctify Your Name, expose such crooks and may they come to repentance or utterly abandon service.

Paul wrote, *"But godliness with contentment is great gain. For we brought nothing into the world, and we can take nothing out of it. But if we have food and clothing, we will be content with that. People who want to get rich fall into temptation and a trap and into many foolish and harmful desires that plunge men into ruin and destruction. For the love of money is a root of all kinds of evil. Some people, eager for money, have wandered from the faith and pierced themselves with many griefs"* (1Timothy 6:6-10).

Chapter 7: The Place of Worship

The following lessons can be drawn from here :

1. Godliness with contentment is great again. Not just any kind of gain but great gain, in this life and in the one to come.
2. We brought nothing into this world and we can take nothing out of it, in the words of Job, *"naked we came and naked we shall depart"*, no matter how hard we toil for the vain things of this world.
3. True godliness is contentment with the basic necessities of life.
4. Those who want to get rich fall into:
   - Temptation
   - A trap
   - Many foolish desires
   - Many harmful desires
   - Are plunged into ruin
   - Are plunged into destruction
   - The love of money is the root of all kinds of evil.

Some eager for money have
1. Wondered from the faith
2. Pierced themselves with many griefs.

As I write this, my heart is exposed. The unholy secret motive and desires are brought to light. This calls for nothing but a deep and radical change in our heart's attitude. Are you eager for wealth? Are you eager for money? Do you desire to get rich? God says you are heading for destruction.

You may desperately want to get rich and one day you shall actually be rich, but those riches may bring about swift destruction. At the end you will realize that your spiritual bankruptcy had been great and that you are after destruction and ruin in the disguise of wealth. May I say that Satan will not mind opening doors for you to become rich as long as wealth keeps you as far from God and as close to destruction as possible. If you can possess apparent joy, and luxury but be far away from the center of God's will and plan, Satan will be happy for he has no other goal but to alienate you from God, be it through *"happiness"* or through pains and sorrow.

I should not be misunderstood here; God wants you to be rich. He desires to bless you. Riches and wealth can come from God. And when they come from God, they do not drag you away from Him but instead draw you closer to Him. However, you do not have to run after the riches, you run after God and His righteousness. You do not have to spend all your time toiling to become rich. Remember that *"The blessing of the LORD brings wealth, without painful toil for it"* (Proverbs 10:22).

The Ruthless Enemy

> *"Then the LORD said to Satan, "Have you considered my servant Job? There is no one on earth like him; he is blameless and upright, a man who fears God and shuns evil. And he still maintains his integrity, though you incited me against him to ruin him without any reason." "Skin for skin!" Satan replied. "A man will give all he has for his own life. But stretch out your hand and strike his flesh and bones, and he will surely curse you to your face"* (Job. 2:3-5).

God's confidence in Job was unwavering. Even after Satan's first wave of deadly attacks, Job maintained his integrity and uprightness in the eyes of God and so God had every reason to boast of him. May we like Job maintain our integrity even after we have lost everything. May we hold on unswervingly to truth, holiness and uprightness without any compromise though we lose all the Lord gave us! May our eyes and thoughts be focused on the Giver and not the gifts, then in all situations we shall stand firm with our heads up!

> *"Skin for skin... a man would give up all he has for his own life".*

May I use this phrase to challenge you in a positive sense. There is a treasure you possess, a priceless treasure – eternal life, which can be found in no one else, but our risen Lord, Christ Jesus. Are you ready to give up everything for your eternal life? Are you ready to give up your position or that business deal or that relationship for your eternal life? In this light, examine your innermost thoughts and the value you give for your life in Christ Jesus. For a man who compromises his integrity for a little gain will give up his salvation for a great gain. Until you reach a point where deep down your heart you are willing not only to lose everything, but also your very life in order to preserve your salvation, you remain an insecure soul. One day the threat of death shall cause you to denounce the One who gave His All so you could live for Him.

A Relentless Foe

Satan never gives up on his targets. He will not give up on you. He may leave you *"until an opportune time"* but during that period of leave, he looks for new ways to attack. After his first attack failed to produce its end, he now took a different approach: getting Job to feel in his bones the pain of serving the Lord. O how many have felt this pain, yet it is their joy of suffering for the sake of the gospel. Many have willingly lain down their lives. Others at the price of their wealth and health have laboured to carry the message of the cross of Calvary across the continents.

> *"So Satan went out from the presence of the Lord and afflicted Job with painful sores from his feet to the top of his head."*

But for the Lord Jesus Christ and His victory over Satan and his host, you and I would remain helpless in the hands of Satan. What cruelty, what mercilessness! If he had the opportunity, Satan would get you and I punished for our allegiance to Christ. He will spare nothing to ensure that we bear on our bodies the pains of serving the Lord. And such pains are not ordinary. If your goal in life is anything but loving and pleasing the Lord, then be sure that one day you will be left with *"no reason"* to follow Him. For surely a day will come when all secondary and tertiary reasons will fly away like chaff in the wind. You will melt before the trials which are about to befall this generation as wax melts before fire if you have ulterior motives in serving the LORD.

If not for the Lord Jesus Christ and His victory on Calvary, we have no ground to resist the devil and his works, our destruction would be swift. He is a tyrant who desires that all follow his course of rebellion against God. But thanks be to God Almighty who has power and wisdom to guard and protect all who respond to His call.

Chapter Eight

Relationships: A Peril or a Blessing?

"His wife said to him, "Are you still holding on to your integrity? Curse God and die!" He replied, "You are talking like a foolish woman. Shall we accept good from God, and not trouble?" In all this, Job did not sin in what he said. When Job's three friends, Eliphaz the Temanite, Bildad the Shuhite and Zophar the Naamathite, heard about all the troubles that had come upon him, they set out from their homes and met together by agreement to go and sympathize with him and comfort him. When they saw him from a distance, they could hardly recognize him; they began to weep aloud, and they tore their robes and sprinkled dust on their heads. Then they sat on the ground with him for seven days and seven nights. No one said a word to him, because they saw how great his suffering was" (Job. 2:9-13).

The relationships you build in times of prosperity and happiness determine your attitude in times of misfortune and sorrow. May I ask you some questions and may you respond in all honesty: What is the basis of your choice of relationships? Are they based on the determination to know God more and be built in Him? May be I went too fast in that question. Let's come back a bit, do you have relationships or you are an island?

I imagine the pain and disappointment that gripped Job's heart as the blaspheming words of the one to whom his soul was united reached his ears.

On whom else could Job have relied for comfort but his wife? But we see her fail woefully in standing beside her husband as a helper. Instead of encouragement came discouragement from her lips. The same lips, which were supposed to uplift a man's soul, were now trying to bring despair. No doubt Satan spared her life, so he could use her to pull down Job's hopes. Was there any use for such a woman by such a man in a time as this? Certainly not!

May I say those Satan will use against you are people in your immediate circle, for their words usually have a great bearing upon your soul either positively or negatively. This means that there is no doubt that a man who has *"Job's wife"* around him will end up cursing God. For such people are willing to *"accept good from God and not evil"*. In times of prosperity, they sing praises; in times of calamity they pronounce curses. If this is your case, it's a pity that your relationships will be but a peril.

May I take you to another category of people: those who live like the people of Laish. In their heydays, they shun the company of others. For some, they do not just have time to waste in building relationships. For what can they gain from such relationships? Haven't they all they need?

> *"So the five men left and came to Laish, where they saw that the people were living in safety, like the Sidonians, unsuspecting and secure. And since their land lacked nothing, they were prosperous. Also, they lived a long way from the Sidonians and had no relationship with anyone else"* (Judges. 18:7).

These people

1. Lived in safety.
2. Were unsuspecting.
3. Were secure
4. Their land lacked nothing
5. Were prosperous.
6. Lived a long way from their nearest neighbor.
7. Had no relationship with anyone else.

Chapter 8: Relationships: A Peril or a Blessing?

Often, people who live as an island find safety and security in their wealth. In their island, they are very prosperous and lack nothing for they ask nothing from anyone. There is nothing they cannot find on their island. For many, it is life on Treasure Island. Such people may be found in the midst of others but are always very distant, millions of miles away from anyone who thinks he is close to them. Though they have relationships with a few people, it is always those of their kind – Liashists and Sidonians. But there is a sad side in this, the Bible says, *"They attacked them with the sword and burned down their city. There was no one to rescue them because they lived a long way from Sidon and had no relationship with anyone else"* (Judges 18:27[b]-28[b]).

Is your misfortune attributed to the fact that you had no solid relationship with anyone? You felt so self-sufficient. When misfortune came knocking at your door, there was no one to help. Maybe you felt ashamed running to those you despised all along when you felt safe and secure. Is there someone who can come to your rescue should misfortune befall you? Do not be quick to answer, weigh it on honest scales and may your heart respond to that question. Have you one to whom you can run for shelter in times of danger? Have you one to whom you can expose your weakness and failures in order to cut the ground from beneath Satan? My cry is that you should hurry to build one such relationship at the least.

David could run to Samuel when he was escaping from Saul who badly wanted to take away his life. What I mean is someone in the household of God. Do not tell me you have a king Achish somewhere among the enemy of God's people to whom you can run. Remember when David ran to Achish, he had to compromise his integrity by pretending to be insane. He was later even willing to attack his own people. It is better to have a servant in the household of God to whom you can run than ten kings in the camp of the enemy. One thing is sure; a man should and must have relationships even though he seems to be self-sufficient.

Do You Have Loyal Friends?

Job had friends who could sympathize with him. They could abandon their daily business for seven days to sit appalled beside their troubled friend. Yes, these friends came to sympathize and to comfort him. They wept and mourned and sat with him where he was. They did not send wealth and things to replace what Job had lost. They did not send money or greeting cards. They came in person and for seven days kept Job company without uttering a word.

Let me ask a question I asked earlier on, but here in a somewhat higher tone, if I may say so. Do you have friends who can sympathize with you in times of trouble? Do you have friends who will be willing to abandon all their daily routine of making money to come and comfort you with their presence? Do you have one who will lie where you lie, sit where you sit, eat where you eat in times of your misfortune? If not, then in the area of relationship you need to improve drastically.

Let me draw your attention to someone in scripture that had such a relationship. It is a story of Lazarus who died and was raised back to life. Read the whole of John 11, meanwhile, we will focus on the verse we quote.

> "*So the sisters sent word to Jesus, "Lord, the one you love is sick"* (John. 11:3).

Do you have a friend whom your family knows about, whom they can call to say something when you are unable to speak? One who knows your secrets? In other words, is there a friend who knows you in and out? Do you have a friend whom your family can run to should danger befall you? Whom your family can count on for moral support at any time? Whom your family recognizes as a real friend? Whom your family can testify that he loves you? Are you determinant in your relationships or you have a superficial friendship which ends in the tennis court, after service, or in cafeteria?

Lazarus' family knew of his relationship with the Lord. They knew He loved him, and could abandon all He was still to do so as to come to Bethany. For Lazarus and for Job relationship was a blessing. What is your case?

We Are Only Humans

> *"After this, Job opened his mouth and cursed the day of his birth"* (Job. 3:1).

Kindly read through Job 3 to get a fuller picture. Until now, in spite of all that happened, Job had proven strong and unwavering; he accepted his lot from the hand of his Maker. Look at these two verses for a moment.

> *"In all this, Job did not sin by charging God with wrongdoing. Shall we accept good from God, and not trouble?"… "In all this, Job did not sin in what he said"* (Job 1:22, 2:10[b]).

Very few people nowadays can bear that kind of testimony. Have our moments of trials not been filled with grumbling, murmuring, questioning and complaining and in all these, sin is never lacking? Do you dare challenge or question the working of God in your life? Do you expect things to go the way you have imagined and so when the course of things is strange to you, you take offense at God?

Well, here is Job allowing despair to creep in. He begins by cursing the day he was born. He regrets why he was born and why he had lived. No matter how strong you are, your strength has limitation. On our own, we shall give up in face of trials. But for the Spirit of grace, we shall all crumble in the face of fiery ordeals. Our human capacities have limitations and as far as the things of God are concerned, they have no place unless rejuvenated by the Spirit of grace.

By His Grace Alone

> *"Think how you have instructed many, how you have strengthened feeble hands. Your words have supported those who stumbled; you have strengthened faltering knees. But now trouble comes to you, and you are discouraged; it strikes you, and you are dismayed"* (Job. 4:3-5).

Here is Job who had encouraged many in their times of distress, instructed many and strengthened the weak. But here comes a moment when he is discouraged.

He sits in dismay and despairs even of life itself. From this, we can conclude that, <u>no one is anything until he has gotten a clear and equal opportunity to be the contrary</u>. Until something has befallen you, it is hard to understand those who face the practicalities of it, though you may be a theoretical expert.

> *"Should not your piety be your confidence and your blameless ways your hope?"* (Job. 4:6)

No! And never! No matter how pure your ways are, no matter how blameless, upright and God fearing you are, place no confidence in these, and never let your hope rely on such. What of the times you will fall or stumble? What of the times you find your hands in the mud? Then you shall have no confidence, no hope. In everything, God alone should be your confidence and hope. He alone is unfailing in holiness and purity. Never let your piety be your confidence. Besides, the Bible says:

> *"All of us have become like one who is unclean, and all our righteous acts are like filthy rags; we all shrivel up like a leaf, and like the wind our sins sweep us away"* (Isaiah 64:6).

> *"Can a mortal be more righteous than God? Can a man be more pure than his Maker? If God places no trust in his servants, if he charges his angels with error, how much more those who live in houses of clay, whose foundations are in the dust, who are crushed more readily than a moth!"* (Job 4:17-19)

We can only rely on God's righteousness and holiness. Are you in despair? Your case is not unique. A mighty man like Job was also in that situation. However, may it be that if you suffer, it should not be because you abandoned the word of the Lord, but like Job you should be able to say:

> *"Then I would still have this consolation— my joy in unrelenting pain— that I had not denied the words of the Holy One"* (Job 6:10).

Your joy should be that you have not turned your back on your Maker, that you have not rejected His word to you in private.

Hope again

Maybe like Job you are saying; *"What strength do I have, that I should still hope? What prospects, that I should be patient?"* (Job 6:11)

Well you have an infinite reserve from which you can draw strength in order to keep hoping. God is the strength of your heart. In Him you shall always find strength to press on. And this should be your prospect, to keep you patient, that God will one day come and vindicate you, that one-day your deliverance shall come and that sorrows last but for a night. All you need do is acknowledge your helplessness without Him, whether you are succeeding or you experience failure. In your heart, the answer to this question which Job asked himself, "Do I have any power to help myself, now that success has been driven from me?" (Vs 13) should be "No!" Apart from Him, there is no power even when success is around me. This again should be your joy that you are still holding fast to the word of God. For if what is happening to you at this moment is from the hand of God, this should be your consolation:

"Blessed is the man whom God corrects; so do not despise the discipline of the Almighty. For he afflicts, but he also consoles; he injures, but his hands also heal. From six calamities he will rescue you; in seven no harm will befall you. In famine he will ransom you from death, and in battle from the stroke of the sword. You will be protected from the lash of the tongue, and need not fear when destruction comes. You will laugh at destruction and famine, and need not fear the beasts of the earth. For you will have a covenant with the stones of the field, and the wild animals will be at peace with you. You will know that your tent is secure; you will take stock of your property and find nothing missing. You will know that your children will be many, and your descendants like the grass of the earth. You will come to the grave in full vigor, like sheaves gathered in season. 'We have examined this, and it is true. So hear it and apply it to yourself'" (Job 5:17-27). When God wounds, He also binds up the wound as we learn from the wound He gives, for He never wounds for pleasure.

Do I mean to say there is no hope for he whose situation is a result of his sins or folly? One who in rebellion to the counsel of the word of God finds himself in a mess? No! In every situation there is still hope. God had made provision for that too, in His infinite love and mercy. But only, in such cases, the lessons are too bitter and the consequences so outstanding. In some cases, you may have to bear the marks of your rebellion and sin for the rest of your earthly life, though after repentance, you stand forgiven. If that your case is a result of sin, *"But if you will look to God and plead with the Almighty, if you are pure and upright, even now he will rouse himself on your behalf and restore you to your rightful place"* (Job 8:5-6).

> *"Yet if you devote your heart to him and stretch out your hands to him, if you put away the sin that is in your hand and allow no evil to dwell in your tent, then you will lift up your face without shame; you will stand firm and without fear. You will surely forget your trouble, recalling it only as waters gone by. Life will be brighter than noonday, and darkness will become like morning. You will be secure, because there is hope; you will look about you and take your rest in safety. You will lie down, with no one to make you afraid, and many will court your favor"* (Job 11:13-19).

Yeah; plead with the Almighty. That is all you can do and all you must do. His love and mercy endure forever. He is ready to restore you to your original position if you return to purity and uprightness. As you purge out your sin, God starts taking care of the things Satan stole from you through your rebellion. Yeah, *"He will yet fill your mouth with laughter and your lips with shouts of joy"* (Job 8:21).

May be you are saying in your heart, *"but why is this still happening to me? I have kept my way pure"*. Shall you not learn what God in His infinite wisdom is preparing you for? Will you question Him? Will you continue to grumble? May be like Job you need to come to the point where you give up all efforts for self-rescue and deliverance, all empty complains and murmuring and say, *"Though I were innocent, I could not answer him; I could only plead with my Judge for mercy"* (Job 9:15). This is because any other thing you do is trying to resist His working in your life. Remember, *"His wisdom is profound, his power is vast. Who has resisted him and come out unscathed?"* (Job 9:4) and *"If it is a matter of strength, he is mighty! And if it is a matter of justice, who will summon him?"* (Job 9:19)

A Faithful Friend

At such a time in Job's life, everyone had misunderstood him, including his closest friends who were willing to go with him as far as he went in this trouble. They too had misinterpreted his misfortune. His wife had failed and now his friends too, not to mention his brothers. In the face of abandonment Job lamented:

> *"A despairing man should have the devotion of his friends, even though he forsakes the fear of the Almighty. But my brothers are as undependable as intermittent streams, as the streams that overflow when darkened by thawing ice and swollen with melting snow, but that cease to flow in the dry season, and in the heat vanish from their channels"* (Job 6:14-17).

> *"My kinsmen have gone away; my friends have forgotten me. My guests and my maidservants count me a stranger; they look upon me as an alien. I summon my servant, but he does not answer, though I beg him with my own mouth. My breath is offensive to my wife; I am loathsome to my own brothers. Even the little boys scorn me; when I appear, they ridicule me. All my intimate friends detest me; those I love have turned against me"* (Job 19:14-19).

That is the best description of human dependence. Though all around you may fail you, there is One who never fails. O! How my heart goes to that little old song.

> *Jesus never fails!* (2x)
> *The man of the world may let you down*
> *But Jesus never fails*
> *Your father will let you down*
> *Your mother will let you down*
> *The man of the world may let you down*
> *But Jesus never fails.*

And you can go on and on singing out the things and people who may let you down and proclaiming the faithfulness of Jesus at all times. May you and

I know this in our hearts, not just in the head and may it be forever engraved in bold. Job seems to have known this only in his head, for his words betrayed him. No matter what comes your way, you can draw infinite strength and consolation from this truth, if written on your heart:

> *"Even now my witness is in heaven; my advocate is on high. My intercessor is my friend as my eyes pour out tears to God; on behalf of a man he pleads with God as a man pleads for his friend"* (Job 16:19-21).

Who is your advocate? Who is your intercessor – friend? Who is your witness? Jesus. Jesus. Jesus. Yes He is your Witness in heaven. He bears testimonies to the weakness of the human flesh *"Therefore, since we have a great high priest who has gone through the heavens, Jesus the Son of God, let us hold firmly to the faith we profess"* (Hebrews 4:14).

Your advocate defends you against the accusations of Satan. While Satan points at your failures, He tells the Father *"O yes, but I died for that weakness too, I paid the full price for his forgiveness, I carried on my body the full punishment for it"*. Your intercessor prays for you without ceasing. He pleads your cause before the Father. On your behalf He pleads with God as a man pleads with his friend.

What truth! What consolation! What comfort! That we may learn to trust Him in all things at all times. May we truly abandon ourselves in His hands, to deal with us as He *"seest meet"*. How I wish you pause for a moment and flow out to Him in songs of worship and thanksgiving.

"As my Eyes Pour out Tears to God"

Often we have kept our eyes dry even when the pain we feel is so intense. We think it is bravery to hold back tears. My brother do you feel pains? Pour out your tears to God again and again and again. There is power in tears, God sees each tear you cry, they are sacrifices unto Him and He records them for a reward in due time. More on that latter!

When No One Understands

There are moments when one thing goes wrong and everything about you is questioned. No one seems to understand what you try to explain. Conclusions are already drawn and the *"instant judges"* of our time have passed a unanimous verdict concerning you. Deep down within, you know your hands are clean, you never compromised. You are being slandered, backbitten, or accused falsely for something you have no idea of, and everyone seems to believe the framed-up stuff. Or maybe a misfortune has come your way, you have lost all you so dearly worked for in all integrity and all the *"quick judges"* can do is to say *"the evil that men do live after them"*. If that is your plight, no matter how great or small it may be, you are not alone.

Job's friends accused him wrongly. One after another, they poured out words which tormented his soul. They said things totally contrary to what God said about Job. Here are some of those false accusations:

> *"Is not your wickedness great? Are not your sins endless? You demanded security from your brothers for no reason; you stripped men of their clothing, leaving them naked. You gave no water to the weary and you withheld food from the hungry, though you were a powerful man, owning land— an honored man, living on it. And you sent widows away empty-handed and broke the strength of the fatherless. That is why snares are all around you, why sudden peril terrifies you"* (Job 22:5-10).

> *"When your children sinned against him, he gave them over to the penalty of their sin"* (Job 8:4).

Some would use Bible verses to show you your sin. What they labor to say is true but in your case it does not apply. There is much insight and truth in what his friends where saying but that did not apply to Job. Some will claim to have received a special vision or word of wisdom or word of knowledge as concerns your situation, yet even they are in error. As far as you are concerned, the only one who knows the truth and can speak on your behalf is the

God of Heaven. Continue to hope in Him, to look up to Him alone. Only He cannot accuse falsely. At such moments, let your soul run after Him at all times of the day.

Envied The Wicked?

> *"Yet you ask him, 'What profit is it to me, and what do I gain by not sinning?'"* (Job 35:3)

> *"Why do the wicked live on, growing old and increasing in power? They see their children established around them, their offspring before their eyes. Their homes are safe and free from fear; the rod of God is not upon them. Their bulls never fail to breed; their cows calve and do not miscarry. They send forth their children as a flock; their little ones dance about. They sing to the music of tambourine and harp; they make merry to the sound of the flute. They spend their years in prosperity and go down to the grave in peace. Yet they say to God, 'Leave us alone! We have no desire to know your ways. Who is the Almighty that we should serve him? What would we gain by praying to him?"* (Job 21:7-15)

Have you regretted the day that you made a commitment to follow Christ? Before you came to Him, all was seemingly fine but now that you are in Him there seems to be trouble all around? You were promised peace, comfort, heydays, gain and every other thing but suffering. Now your experience is the contrary – you have nothing but suffering?

I have always wondered when I hear people being invited to Christ on the basis of prosperity, security etc. They say, *"Come to Christ and all your problems will be gone"*. Yet for some, it only doubles, theirs begin when they came to Christ. You long for days you lived in apparent safety, your businesses were flourishing, and you were unrestricted in all you did. But today, the Spirit of God won't allow you do certain things you long to do. Your life is that of battling with God.

Asaph, the Psalmist had this same problem when he declared:

> "*But as for me, my feet had almost slipped; I had nearly lost my foothold. For I envied the arrogant when I saw the prosperity of the wicked. They have no struggles; their bodies are healthy and strong. They are free from the burdens common to man; they are not plagued by human ills*" (Psalm 73:2-15).

In his trouble, he too envied the wicked and this almost caused him to backslide. There are things in this life, which you can never understand, things which defy mere reasoning or logic. The Bible says judgment begins in the household of God, but theirs is being stored up. Only in the presence of God through His word and Spirit can you understand this. As the Psalmist said,

> "*When I tried to understand all this, it was oppressive to me till I entered the sanctuary of God; then I understood their final destiny. Surely you place them on slippery ground; you cast them down to ruin. How suddenly are they destroyed, completely swept away by terrors! As a dream when one awakes, so when you arise, O Lord, you will despise them as fantasies. When my heart was grieved and my spirit embittered, I was senseless and ignorant; I was a brute beast before you. Yet I am always with you; you hold me by my right hand. You guide me with your counsel, and afterward you will take me into glory. Who have I in heaven but you? And earth has nothing I desire besides you. My flesh and my heart may fail, but God is the strength of my heart and my portion forever. Those who are far from you will perish; you destroy all who are unfaithful to you. But as for me, it is good to be near God. I have made the Sovereign LORD my refuge; I will tell of all your deeds*"
> (Psalm 73:16-28).

That is their lot, and it shall come to them. Like Asaph may you keep near to God and remain faithful to Him. Some people totally shun suffering and nothing will cause them to accept it as part of the Christian race. They prefer to exchange their piety for a moment of pleasure or comfort. To this I say No! Not me but the word.

> "*Be careful that no one entices you by riches; do not let a large bribe turn you aside. Would your wealth or even all your mighty efforts sustain you so you would not be in distress? Do not long for the night, to drag people away*

from their homes. Beware of turning to evil, which you seem to prefer to affliction" (Job 36:18-21).

Could it not be that the trouble that has come your way is that God wants to turn you away from calamity? He has sent His storm to turn you away from the wrong path you are treading. It is written,

> *"For God does speak—now one way, now another— though man may not perceive it. In a dream, in a vision of the night, when deep sleep falls on men as they slumber in their beds, he may speak in their ears and terrify them with warnings, to turn man from wrongdoing and keep him from pride, to preserve his soul from the pit, his life from perishing by the sword. Or a man may be chastened on a bed of pain with constant distress in his bones, so that his very being finds food repulsive and his soul loathes the choicest meal He redeemed my soul from going down to the pit, and I will live to enjoy the light.' "God does all these things to a man— twice, even three times- to turn back his soul from the pit, that the light of life may shine on him"*
> (Job 33:14-20, 28-30).

> *"But those who suffer he delivers in their suffering; he speaks to them in their affliction. "He is wooing you from the jaws of distress to a spacious place free from restriction, to the comfort of your table laden with choice food"*
> (Job 36:15-16).

So stop fighting with the God of Heaven, stop persisting in your own way and

> *"Submit to God and be at peace with him; in this way prosperity will come to you. Accept instruction from his mouth and lay up his words in your heart. If you return to the Almighty, you will be restored: If you remove wickedness far from your tent and assign your nuggets to the dust, your gold of Ophir to the rocks in the ravines, then the Almighty will be your gold, the choicest silver for you. Surely then you will find delight in the Almighty and will lift up your face to God. You will pray to him, and he will hear you, and you will fulfill your vows. What you decide on will be done, and light will shine on your ways"* (Job 22:21-28).

Chapter Nine

Holding Fast

"As long as I have life within me, the breath of God in my nostrils, my lips will not speak wickedness, and my tongue will utter no deceit. I will never admit you are in the right; till I die, I will not deny my integrity. I will maintain my righteousness and never let go of it; my conscience will not reproach me as long as I live" (Job 27:3-6).

Have you ever tried to screw up something with a worn out bolt? How did it look? When the bolt was new, it could fit well and hold tight but after continuous usage, it wore out and lost its *"value"*. Trials and storms too can wear us out depending on the way we react to them. Certain attitudes are very dangerous at any time of your life, most of all during trying moments. The one who faces trials needs the whole of his emotional, psychological, and spiritual strength in order to come out with his head lifted high. Thus everything must be done to conserve this energy.

Like any other form of energy, these forms too can be dissipated, and our aim is to keep to the very minimum, any energy loses. The greater the energy loss, the less the energy put into effective use and vice versa. You will want to improve your *"productivity"* in time of trials. How can you be useful to God, your environment, and to yourself during trials? That is how you can ensure that you walk with your head high above the troubled waters. We shall begin by identifying the channels of energy loss and see how we can minimize them.

1. **Murmuring:** A person who murmurs already opens the way to psychological defeat. Murmuring is one of the ways through which psychological energy is lost. A man who loses psychological energy is left with just two sources to keep him going. A man who murmurs sees everything wrong with God, man, and himself. Murmuring easily gets you mad at people, and again here useful energy is wasted.
2. **Grumbling:** A man who grumbles is always at war with himself and "a house at war with itself cannot stand". Now part of the energy needed to resist your enemy is wasted in something that could be avoided. Further, a man who grumbles places himself against God. Here too, useful energy is wasted fighting God.

"These men are grumblers and faultfinders; they follow their own evil desires; they boast about themselves and flatter others for their own advantage" (Jude 16).

"And do not grumble, as some of them did—and were killed by the destroying angel" (1 Corinthians 10:10).

You see, grumbling is a sin like any other and it brings God against you. Now if the One who should be your strength stands against you, what is your lot? Of course, destruction.

3. **Complaining:** A man who complains in times of trials questions God's sovereignty. You should understand that God made you for His pleasure and He loves you. You should also understand that He takes no pleasure in evil (Psalm 5:4) and so if your suffering were evil He will immediately come to your rescue. Nothing saps spiritual energy like complaining. The man who complains runs dry spiritually. With your spiritual energy sapped, you cannot fight the spiritual battle with only psychological or emotional energy.

Once you begin murmuring, grumbling and complaining, you realize you can no longer hold fast to the truth you know. In all these, your lips utter sinful statements, your conscience begins reproaching you. In whatever situation, your desire should always be like Job's and that should be your resolve, to come out victorious in every test or trial.

Never allow yourself to be at war with you. Keep your conscience on the right. Maintain your righteousness. I'm quite sure you already know that Satan will always want to take advantage of your low moments. At such times, he makes offers, *"if only you will just do this, the storm would cease"*. *"Look, what would it take to manipulate this figure so you can have some extra bugs? Don't you need money"*? And if you respond to his suggestions you compromise your righteousness and you can never be the same again, your conscience is sold to the devil. Your resolve should be that *"In every high and stormy gale, my anchor holds within the Vail"*.

Yeah! Holding onto your integrity and righteousness! In times of storms do not break your covenant with God. For are not the storms there to test the genuineness of your commitments and resolve? Breaking them means you are defeated already.

The Glory Of The Storm

> *"I know that you can do all things; no plan of yours can be thwarted. You asked, 'Who is this that obscures my counsel without knowledge?' Surely I spoke of things I did not understand, things too wonderful for me to know. "You said, 'Listen now, and I will speak; I will question you, and you shall answer me.' My ears had heard of you but now my eyes have seen you. Therefore I despise myself and repent in dust and ashes"* (Job 42:2-6).

1. Storms are there to bring us to a position as this. We believe God for what He is, as revealed in His word. We come to know that none of His plans can be thwarted: neither by you nor by the enemy. The storms bring us to humble positions, where we acknowledge God's sovereignty and our fallibility. Here we see Job acknowledging God's power in a lowly state.

2. Job was able to hear God's voice audibly. Until now, Job had only heard of God but now he could hear God directly through no intermediary.
3. Job saw God with his own eyes

"*My ears had heard of you but now my eyes have seen you*" (Job 42:5).

What a blessing to behold Him face to face. It is our goal, our longing, and our expectation that one-day we shall behold His glorious face and worship Him.

4. Job was made a priest: In the whole Bible, Job was the very first person to offer burnt offerings on behalf of another, to atone for the sins of another. Until now, he had done it only for his household; God gave him this privilege that no one else could have.

"After Job had prayed for his friends, the LORD made him prosperous again and gave him twice as much as he had before. All his brothers and sisters and everyone who had known him before came and ate with him in his house. They comforted and consoled him over all the trouble the LORD had brought upon him, and each one gave him a piece of silver and a gold ring. The LORD blessed the latter part of Job's life more than the first. He had fourteen thousand sheep, six thousand camels, a thousand yoke of oxen and a thousand donkeys. And he also had seven sons and three daughters. The first daughter he named Jemimah, the second Keziah and the third Keren-Happuch. Nowhere in all the land were there found women as beautiful as Job's daughters, and their father granted them an inheritance along with their brothers. After this, Job lived a hundred and forty years; he saw his children and their children to the fourth generation. And so he died, old and full of years" (Job 42:10-17).

How good is our God, how generous, how gracious is the Lover of our souls! My heart goes out to the statement *"the Lord blessed the later part of Job's life more than the first"*. Now what is the later part of Job's life? Of course his life after the storms. I trust you know that this was not some kind of magical restoration where everything just came at once. As Job was made humble, as he applied the lesson learnt in the storm, the blessings of the God of heaven were

Chapter 9: Holding Fast

poured forth into his lap. Job who was once an outcast (during the storm) now had people coming to comfort him. Now, what was the magnitude of *"more – than the first?"* The Bible lets us know it was two – two times everything Job had.

God will also restore with a bonus everything we lose in times of trials, when we cooperate with Him and come out victorious from such moments. Everything the devil has stolen from you, God will restore. As you trust Him, He shall pour it into your lap to overflowing. My brother, my sister, though yours may not be immediately, it surely will be. Though it may not come in the same magnitude, it surely shall come. Though it may not be in this life here on earth, God will not forget your reward – the crown of life reserved only for those who have gone through trials and persevered and remained faithful to God:

> *"Do not be afraid of what you are about to suffer. I tell you, the devil will put some of you in prison to test you, and you will suffer persecution for ten days. Be faithful, even to the point of death; and I will give you the crown of life"* (Revelation 2:10).

The names Job gave his three daughters after the trials have a great bearing and significance to us. It is not for nothing that God allowed those names to be mentioned here.

He named his first daughter Jemimah. Jemimah means dove and what does a dove signify but God's peace and God's anointing. The later part of Job's life, I believe was full of the peace of God, as the Holy Spirit overshadowed his life with the great anointing of the Father. If you and I shall go through the trials God brings our way victoriously then His anointing shall come upon us in great measures.

He named his second daughter Keziah, which means *"Cassia"*.

Cassia is the (medical) laxative pulp obtained from the pods of Cassia fistula, a cinnamon in the East Indies. Surely, Job recognized the storm as medicine to his soul. And that is just what trials are, medicines to those who go through them. The third he named Keren – Happuch. Keren – Happuch means the horn of Antimony, which is a beautifier. O! How true it is that those who pass through storms victoriously came out with a beauty of the Spirit that others know not. Yeah, they come out with the beauty of *"the inner self, the unfading beauty of a gentle and quiet spirit, which is of great worth in God's sight"* (I Peter 3:4).

Now I want you to see the order in which Job realized the glories of the storm.

1. The anointing
2. Medicine
3. Beauty

May you know that when the Holy Spirit comes upon a life, He comes as medicine to both the body and soul of that individual. He comes (the Dove) with healing in his wings, to heal the heart that has been broken, to heal the broken emotions and mend the wreckage from the storm. After He heals, He beautifies and this beauty becomes evident to all who pass by. O I almost forgot to mention long life. After the storm Job lived a hundred and forty years. The one who once looked like a dead man; a living corpse was transformed into a strong and robust body. Glory be to God!

Part Three

The Life of Jeremiah

In the previous section, we saw Job before his trials, Job in the midst of trials, and Job after his trials. Those trials became glories to him. Before that, we saw Joseph the young man with a dream, how he too went through trials and how for him, they became glories too. Well, one may consider that these two people had *"secular visions"*. In this section we shall look at the life of Jeremiah, a young man with an authentic calling from God, with an unusual anointing, but who faced trials too.

Some people who do not identify themselves with the first two cases may do so with Jeremiah's. You have a clear calling from God, you have responded to it. You have abandoned all for His sake. The glories and luxuries of this world mean nothing to you. All that counts to you is God, yet life has not been at its best. You have faced one problem after another; you have faced daily rejection from those who belong to the God who has sent you. As we examine the life of this great Prophet, may the Spirit of truth speak with conviction and power to your heart!

I wrote the first two parts of this book two years when I first received the inspiration before writing the part three. I had no idea of including the life of Jeremiah. In fact, I never thought of it until it came like a flash when I started writing some weeks ago. I want to trust that God who has caused me to include this section has at least an individual He wants to touch in His own way. My prayer is that this book should get into the hands of that one to whom our Father in Heaven wants to render ministry. If you ever went through the prophets, you would realize no prophet suffered like Jeremiah, and few had such outstanding flourishing prophetic ministry. The first time I went through my Bible, I fell in love with Jeremiah because of his courage, zeal for his God and all what he went through and so he became my most favorite prophet. He loved his people, yet did not compromise his ministry. Father, grant us to learn new things from these pages, open our spirits that we may truly be receptive and responsive to Your voice.

Chapter Ten

Where He Came From

I want us to take a brief look at the background of the man we are about to study, this mighty prophet of God. Well, not too much is said directly about where he came from, but in searching other parts of scripture, we can use the clue given us here.

> *"The words of Jeremiah son of Hilkiah, one of the priests at Anathoth in the territory of Benjamin. The word of the LORD came to him in the thirteenth year of the reign of Josiah son of Amon king of Judah, ³ and through the reign of Jehoiakim son of Josiah king of Judah, down to the fifth month of the eleventh year of Zedekiah son of Josiah king of Judah, when the people of Jerusalem went into exile"* (Jeremiah 1:1-3).

This is the only information given about his family background, the son of Hilkiah the priest. Let's take a look at who Hilkiah really was. If you read through 2 Kings 22 and 23, you will find that Hilkiah is mentioned in two forms – Hilkiah the high priest (22:4, 22:8, 23:4) and Hilkiah the priest (22:10, 12, 14). This means that it could be the same person or two separate people. But taking a keen look at chapter 22:8 and 10 reveals that it is the same person, since the high priest who found the book in verse 8 is the priest who gave Shaphan the book as reported in verse 10.

This Hilkiah the priest lived during the reign of Josiah and the one referred to as Jeremiah's father also lived during this time, and probably had given birth to young Jeremiah whom God called. If you read through 2 Chronicles 34, you will find this same interchanging use of high priest and priest with respect to Hilkiah. Though some Bible scholars think they were two different people, I believe it is the same person whom the Bible tells us was the father of Jeremiah who lived in Anathoth. Now Anathoth was a city of Benjamin assigned to the priests by Joshua the mighty general of the Israelite army.

Josiah began his reign at 8, very young and by the time he was 20 – the 12th year of his reign he began to purge Judah and Jerusalem of high places. In the thirteenth year of his reign at age 21, God decided to raise a young prophet Jeremiah to confront Israel with her sin. So Jeremiah was called a year after Josiah began his reforms. Thus we see that Jeremiah was a young man, son of a priest who was involved in the reformation process being carried out by the young king. A young king was to work with a young prophet. May God raise in our days, groups of young people who will be totally committed to Him, to carry out reforms in His house. It is time for young men to rise up to take the lead in the mighty things God is ready to do in this generation. May He find willing hearts and hands and lips to serve our King Jesus.

In Bible times, men of God labored to bring up their children in God's ministry. What is happening to the children of gospel ministers today? Are they not the ones dragging into mud the Holy Name of our Lord? Shall we say the leaders of the Church of today have failed to bring up their children with a vision for God? It is true that the best way to prepare one's children for ministry is by being totally committed to God without neglecting the duty of a parent. Hilkiah was totally caught up with the reforms that were being carried out. He led the repairs of the temple. He found the Book of the Law and sent it through Shaphan the secretary to the king.

I want to believe that had any of the corrupt priests or officials found the book, they would have hidden it so that Judah would continue to live in ignorance of the law. He led the team, which went to inquire of the Lord. Are you a gospel minister? Will you hold on to the truth and to your wholehearted commitment to God and His purposes in this generation where everyone is running after gains? Will you draw your children's attention to God and His interests?

May be you are just a young man with no religious background. What I mean is that neither your parents nor your grandparents have ever known the Lord. You are the first believer in your family. Does that mean you have no place? For sure God wants to use you as He does anyone else. You can begin shaping the future for your generation to come by giving yourself totally to God. That is the only way of security. Take care of God's needs and He will take good care of yours. Sounds funny?

The best way God could reward Hilkiah in this life was to raise up his son in the caliber of a prophet. Do you still remember David? His commitment to God continued to reap benefits for his generation long after he had died. Many a time God told his descendants *"for the sake of My servant David"*. On the other hand, do you see the disaster Jeroboam brought upon his descendants? Nothing we do in this Christian life is neutral; it shall either positively or negatively affect our descendants.

The Circumstances Surrounding His Calling

During the reign of Josiah, the only one through whom the whole of Judah could inquire of the Lord was Huldah the prophetess. God foresaw that Josiah would be the last king to reign in righteousness. Thus he knew the difficult task that awaited anyone who would proclaim His word. Of course you can bear with me that no woman could have been equal to the task Jeremiah was called to. As Jeremiah came into the scene, Huldah gradually went out of scene. It's like Jeremiah took over her ministry. Jeremiah's more than 40 years of ministry were done mostly during the reign of kings who all forsook God to run after idols.

Though when Josiah began his reforms, most people pledged a lip allegiance to the covenants he made with them, they however continued in their godlessness, thus the task of confronting these people with their sin and turning them back to God was a particularly difficult one. Likewise anyone being called into the ministry today faces such a task. You'll have to stand up against the hypocrisy and apostasy taught on many a pulpit today. You'll have to speak up for your God, holding to the true standards of the Bible which many in their deception consider outdated. The ministry is not a place for people who have no other means to earn a living; it is not a profession but a calling. No doubt those without the call are taking it as a moneymaking industry. God will bring all such to account and judgement.

The Authenticity of His Call

> "*The word of the LORD came to me, saying, 'Before I formed you in the womb I knew you, before you were born I set you apart; I appointed you as a prophet to the nations*" (Jeremiah 1:4-5).

If you read through the prophets, no one took up the prophetic ministry because he had nothing to do. God called each prophet for a particular mission. Jeremiah's call was an authentic call from God. Later, no matter what happened to him, he could look back and be certain that God had called him to this challenging service. What I want to bring out is this: If you are a minister facing trials, flames, and storms in your ministry, you can always look back and draw from the knowledge that God called you to this. This is what will keep you in integrity when all seems to be going wrong.

When others will be compromising here and there for financial gains or material favor, you shall stand alone and be sure that the One who called you to this service is with you. If you are not sure of this then you shall be griped by a sense of insecurity and will decide to join the popular trend. How many are out there in *"the ministry"* claiming *"the Lord told me, the Lord showed me"* meanwhile the Lord never told them anything in the first place, and they were never sent.

> "*Then the LORD said to me, "The prophets are prophesying lies in my name. I have not sent them or appointed them or spoken to them. They are prophesying to you false visions, divinations, idolatries and the delusions of their own minds. I did not send these prophets, yet they have run with their message; I did not speak to them, yet they have prophesied*" (Jeremiah 14:14, 23:21).

Am I talking just about false prophets? Are there not false teachers, false pastors, false apostles, false evangelists, false healers everywhere in the world today? Such people preach lies, the truth is kept aside and myths of prosperity and hyper grace doctrine remain the theme of their massages. From their massages you can always identify them. God totally dissociates Himself from such people. If only those they are leading astray would take time to listen, they would hear God crying out *"I have not sent them"*.

But you probably are sure of your calling. You can look back at the day or period or event during which God drew your attention to His call and you responded wholeheartedly without reservation, yet all has not been easy. All you need is to trust the One who called you into His glorious service. Though the glories might not be evident, they shall one day come. We shall see how Jeremiah coped with this.

Your Limitations – God's Opportunity

From Moses down to Saul, Samson, Gideon and of course Jeremiah, the response to God's call has always been first of all, seeing their shortcomings or limitations. In the case we are studying, his limitation was that of his age:

> *"Ah, Sovereign LORD,"* I said, *"I do not know how to speak; I am only a child"* (Jeremiah 1:6).

Usually the task God calls us to is far too great for anyone to accomplish and the normal human tendency is to turn to the inability. Jeremiah knew the kind of people he was called to confront, he saw the impossibility of the call and *"turned it down"*. How many young people have rejected God's call on the basis of their age? We all in one way or another have been afraid somehow to speak up for God, though He has asked us again and again. We have been afraid to speak against the old prophets and priest who have long been in the vineyard even before we were born.

Do you feel inadequate for the task God has called you to? Already you have genuine excuses and authentic limitations you think will hinder God from using you? I want you to know that throughout Bible history, such limitations have always been welcome by God, they have been opportunities for Him to demonstrate His infinite wisdom, power, and grace. In Jeremiah's case, this was God's response.

> "*But the LORD said to me, 'Do not say, "I am only a child." You must go to everyone I send you to and say whatever I command you. Do not be afraid of them, for I am with you and will rescue you,' declares the LORD. Then the LORD reached out his hand and touched my mouth and said to me, 'Now, I have put my words in your mouth'*" (Jeremiah 1:7-9).

What comfort this should bring to the troubled soul. All you need to do is go where He is sending you. Maybe you are already there, then you are just at the right place. His word to you now is *"do not be afraid of them (the heathen, the devil, the storms, your weaknesses), for I am with you (wherever you go, whatever you do at all times) and will rescue you (from danger, from death, from the enemy)"*. See the Lord touching you at the point of your weakness, both those you are aware of and those you are unaware of. God is reaching out to you right now and putting His strength at the point of your weakness. Paul said, *"I will glory in my weaknesses"* why? Because in them God's strength is made perfect.

A call Against the Trend

> "'*See, today I appoint you over nations and kingdoms to uproot and tear down, to destroy and overthrow, to build and to plant…*' *This is what the LORD said to me: 'Go and stand at the gate of the people, through which the kings of Judah go in and out; stand also at all the other gates of Jerusalem'*" (Jeremiah 1:10, 17:19).

Jeremiah's ministry was given him at a time when evil had crept into the Israelite community. Idolatry was so common and to find a man who ran after righteousness was like finding Ivory where elephants have never been. God Himself challenged Jeremiah who was so burdened for his people to see them pardoned by God:

Chapter 10: Where He Came From

> *"Go up and down the streets of Jerusalem, look around and consider, search through her squares. If you can find but one person who deals honestly and seeks the truth, I will forgive this city"* (Jeremiah 5:1).

I am quite sure disappointment ran down the face of Jeremiah as he searched the streets in vain, looking for just a single man who dealt honestly. To his utmost disappointment, there was none in all of Judah. Both the poor and the rich had become corrupt, the leaders were moving along the same road as the people, those required to teach the others the ways of God were themselves a bunch of dishonest people. God's commission to Jeremiah clearly expressed the kind of task and challenge he was to face.

A child had been appointed against nations and kingdoms, to uproot, to tear down, to destroy, and to overthrow the works of Satan both in the lives of the people and in the nation, and to plant the seeds of God and build altars for his God everywhere.

Has God called you to such a task? Of course, anyone who takes sides with God has much in the supposed house of God to uproot, tear down, destroy and overthrow, for instance, human tradition which has crept into the center of God's house and is being exalted even above the word of God. You have much of the world which has been allowed to sit in the pew for so long, to tear down and destroy from the church. There are sins which have become *"sins for Christians"* and (some of) the leaders are okay with that but God has called you to expose. The sermons in that congregation for decades have only mentioned God's grace but now God is calling you to preach His justice and holiness and so members have risen up against you purporting that you are a legalist. The sins which have been pampered God is calling you to hammer.

Some traditions, which have become laws in the congregation, God is calling you to despise, and everyone seems to rise against you. The very people you were called to shepherd have become wolves tearing you apart. Now to you, He says, *"Get yourself ready! Stand up, do not be terrified, today I have made you a fortified city, an iron pillar and a bronze wall...."*

While you admit the task is difficult, God says, *"Yes! But I have equipped you for all this. Stand your ground and you shall emerge undefeated. They shall fight or better still, they are fighting against you but will never overcome you"*. Why? Simply because God and you are the majority and are on the winning side. Who shall not take sides with the Victor who guarantees victory?

Chapter Eleven

Hypocrites in the House

"This is the word that came to Jeremiah from the LORD: "Stand at the gate of the LORD's house and there proclaim this message: "hear the word of the LORD, all you people of Judah who come through these gates to worship the LORD. This is what the LORD Almighty, the God of Israel, says: Reform your ways and your actions, and I will let you live in this place. Do not trust in deceptive words and say, "This is the temple of the LORD, the temple of the LORD, the temple of the LORD!" If you really change your ways and your actions and deal with each other justly, if you do not oppress the alien, the fatherless or the widow and do not shed innocent blood in this place, and if you do not follow other gods to your own harm, then I will let you live in this place, in the land I gave your forefathers for ever and ever. But look, you are trusting in deceptive words that are worthless. " 'Will you steal and murder, commit adultery and perjury, burn incense to Baal and follow other gods you have not known, and then come and stand before me in this house, which bears my Name, and say, "We are safe"-safe to do all these detestable things? Has this house, which bears my Name, become a den of robbers to you? But I have been watching! declares the LORD" (Jeremiah 7:1-11).

Thank God for those in the assemblies who mean business with God. They are not there to play church but take seriously the things of God and the word of the Lord which is preached in power and conviction. But the sad thing is that in many congregations, the majority of the people do not mean any business with God. Day after day, year after year, they are there to play church, just looking for some place where they can make noise and be heard. They are the ones rising against you because of your emphasis on holiness and purity. They are the ones slandering you, speaking maliciously about you. They are the ones writing petitions upon petitions against you. Show me a church were pastors are constantly being changed and you have seen one packed full of hypocrites who are afraid of the truth, in fact, who hate to be confronted with God's holiness and Christian honesty and integrity.

My brethren, in spite of the opposition, do not give up, continue to preach repentance, and continue to make the house uncomfortable for those who won't go with the truth. Continue to confront them with God's words and truth. Is it not better to speak the word of God and be taken for an enemy than to have God as a terror to you? How many churches lie in ruins today because the minister did not confront the people with their sins? God spoke and they rejected the word because they wanted to be at peace with the unholy members of their congregation.

As you allow hypocrites to find shelter in your church because of fear of man, be sure you are laying the foundations for ruin and destruction of your ministry. For surely a day will come when God will *"pack His things and leave"* and give you time and space to feel free with the hypocrites you have granted refuge for too long. God is always on their lips but far from their hearts, as distant as the furthest star is from the earth.

Though Jeremiah was opposed, he preached the truth - God's holiness and justice. He accepted being on the *"other side of the battle"* – the Victor's side. Let it be your resolve to stand without compromising and to hold fast to that which God called you and yours shall be the blessings of unceasing communion and fellowship with the Spirit of truth and the God of all holiness.

Chapter 11: Hypocrites in the House

God's Hand of Mercy

> *"Therefore this is what the LORD says: 'If you repent, I will restore you that you may serve me; if you utter worthy, not worthless, words, you will be my spokesman. Let this people turn to you, but you must not turn to them'"* (Jeremiah 15:19).

How often, as human beings, do we err? How often do we want to be on the popular side? Very few have stood out uncompromisingly in perilous times. And is the minister any different? Though many do expect extraordinary things from the minister of the Word, we must all acknowledge they too are mere humans. The temptations faced by the ordinary believer are the same they face and in a greater measure.

Surely, Jeremiah spoke from experience when he said, *"The heart is deceitful above all things and beyond cure. Who can understand it?"* (Jeremiah 17:9). He saw how his heart gradually turned to the people. He did not want to stand alone against the odds. In simple terms, we find the mighty prophet Jeremiah a backslider. He had been afraid of the people and in an effort to be at peace with them withheld the word of the Lord and spoke what pleased the people, what their ears wanted to hear.

Paul in his counsel to the young minister, Timothy, said

> *"Preach the Word; be prepared in season and out of season; correct, rebuke and encourage—with great patience and careful instruction. For the time will come when men will not put up with sound doctrine. Instead, to suit their own desires, they will gather around them a great number of teachers to say what their itching ears want to hear. They will turn their ears away from the truth and turn aside to myths"* (2 Timothy 4:2-4).

Let us outline some of the instructions found in these verses.

"Preach the word... correct, rebuke and encourage"

Here, we see three clearly mentioned qualities that were to be found in his preaching. So a wholesome minister has to correct, rebuke, and encourage. Now if the whole sermon of an individual is packed with encouragement such that Sunday after Sunday he preaches encouragement with little or no corrections and rebukes, he is not preaching the whole counsel of God. He is somehow compromising, hence is a backslider. For is it not written, *"All Scripture is God-breathed and is useful for teaching, rebuking, correcting, and training in righteousness."* (2Timothy 3:16)?

Now when a man begins to rationalize the word of God, be sure that he is turning against God. From Paul's counsel to Timothy, we bring out the following:

- Keep your head in all situations. No matter what is happening, do not go insane to the extent that you start taking sides with those who oppose the truth. Do not lose your head, but keep your senses intact. No matter the opposition and persecution from those who reject the truth, never get mad.
- Endure hardship. Stand firm and persist and go through in times of storms and flames. When trials come, do not give in or give up. Stand your ground. If you do not, you shall give in to those who stand against the truth. Yeah, if you don't endure hardship, there is nothing left but to compromise. Do not negotiate the truth of God for some kind of comfort. No one who holds on to the truth finds it easy. Think about our glorious Lord, think about Paul, and think about Timothy who was martyred because he spoke up against idolatry, think of Stephen. The list can continue. So endure the hardship you have because of the truth.
- Discharge all the duties of your ministry. Not some, not those that give you a good face, not those that make you popular but all the duties, including the ones which put you at war with those who won't move along in truth and holiness.

In 2 Timothy 4:3-4, Paul was actually forewarning Timothy that if the goal of his ministry was to satisfy the heart of man, if his aim was to please man, then he had to be sure that one day he will stop preaching the truth and turn over to myths, giving the people what they want to hear. And that is just what is happening nowadays. People gather around preachers who will pamper their sin and tell them those things which will help them cover up their sins. And if your aim is money or fame, you shall surely join the trend.

I believe at this stage in Jeremiah's life, this is the trap he fell into. Did God abandon? No, God invited him to repent and be restored. Our God is a God who gives a second chance. If you have erred by compromising the truth of God, refusing to warn the people of their wickedness because you want to be at peace with them, God is calling you right now to repent and be restored. Don't you hear this invitation? Please do not stray any further. Reach out and touch God's hand of mercy, which is now stretched out for you. The problem is not that you compromised – you turn to the people. All you need do is to turn back to God. Do not take sides with the people but let them come to you – to your side-which is God's side.

Trusting in Rough Times

> *"But blessed is the man who trusts in the LORD, whose confidence is in him. He will be like a tree planted by the water that sends out its roots by the stream. It does not fear when heat comes; its leaves are always green. It has no worries in a year of drought and never fails to bear fruit"*
> (Jeremiah 17:7-8).

The very first thing a minister should build is confidence on the promises of God. Usually again and again, God gives us comforting words during tough times. They are always a confirmation of His initial words at the time of our calling. Again and again He keeps on reminding us of His presence. To Jeremiah, His words of assurance were:

> *"Today I have made you a fortified city, an iron pillar and a bronze wall to stand against the whole land—against the kings of Judah, its officials, its*

> *priests and the people of the land. They will fight against you but will not overcome you, for I am with you and will rescue you," declares the LORD'"* (Jeremiah 1:18, 19).

> *"I will make you a wall to this people, a fortified wall of bronze; they will fight against you but will not overcome you, for I am with you to rescue and save you," declares the LORD. "I will save you from the hands of the wicked and redeem you from the grasp of the cruel"* (Jeremiah 15:20, 21).

You should also have the confidence that God has equipped you for the task and that His presence shall always be with you. This is what brings down the blessings of God upon an individual – the ability to trust in Him during rough and tough times. The individual is in constant and continuous communion with heaven. A tree planted by the water – always in contact with water, does not fear when heat comes. Evergreen leaves have no worries in years of drought, and never fail to bear fruits. The same goes for the one who trusts in the Lord.

Similarly, a minister of the word who trusts in God always receives strength from Him, is always spiritually replenished, is always confident and has no fear of storms or flames. His ministry always flourishes. He is always at peace within even when there are no evidences of God's blessings and favor and presence. He always bears fruits. That will be our lot if we learn to trust even when called against the tides.

Again here, I believe Jerimiah spoke out of his experience when he had repented of his backsliding. He began learning how to trust the Lord and sooner began seeing and reaping the benefits of a life of trust – simple trust. Thus, nothing could hold him back from expressing these benefits of trusting in God. In the previous verses, he expressed the doom that befalls he who trusts in man, who turns from God to take sides with man. Again here he spoke from the bitter experience he had during the time of his backsliding.

> *"This is what the LORD says: "Cursed is the one who trusts in man, who depends on flesh for his strength and whose heart turns away from the LORD. He will be like a bush in the wastelands; he will not see prosperity when it*

comes. He will dwell in the parched places of the desert, in a salt land where no one lives" (Jeremiah 17: 5,6).

What contrast! What extremes. But that's what it is.

Opposition from Fallen Priests and False Prophets

"¹When the priest Pashhur son of Immer, the chief officer in the temple of the LORD, heard Jeremiah prophesying these things, ² he had Jeremiah the prophet beaten and put in the stocks at the Upper Gate of Benjamin at the LORD's temple" (Jeremiah 20:1-2).

"⁷The priests, the prophets and all the people heard Jeremiah speak these words in the house of the LORD.⁸ But as soon as Jeremiah finished telling all the people everything the LORD had commanded him to say, the priests, the prophets and all the people seized him and said, 'You must die!'" (Jeremiah 26:7-8)

"Then the prophet Hananiah took the yoke off the neck of the prophet Jeremiah and broke it" (Jeremiah 28:10).

Every Christian finds it normal if he is persecuted for his faith and commitment to truth by those who have never known the truth, those who have never been enlightened. For such in most cases act under the influence of Satan and his host, though permitted by God to refine our faith and make it solid. You thank God for allowing the persecution to come your way and often you wake up with eager expectation for the results that the persecution brings. It becomes a totally different story when those who were supposed to hold your hands along this rough-narrow road are seeking your downfall. Men robbed of their godly vision, men who once were on fire for God but gradually drifted from the truth for the pursuit of gain. Due to rebellion to God's will, such men have been stripped of the Spirit's fire and power. Such a case is most painful but in it all, God is there to hold your hand.

The first outright opposition to Jeremiah's message came from a supposed priest, Pashhur, who was involved in the offering of daily sacrifice in the temple. His father also earned a living from the temple. Do not expect to find it easy with people who earned a living from ministry throughout life. If your message will send away their costumers, they prefer you carry away that message. They can't bear seeing the people go and experience a drop in their income. They can't bear seeing the people enlightened and so be released from the financial bondage in which their ministers have placed them. And such people rise up against the truth. This reminds me of the great apostle Paul in Ephesus, when the silver smiths rose up against him because the message was cutting down their income. A similar thing happened to Paul and Silas in Phillipi when they delivered the slave girl from familiar spirits. Beatings and imprisonment was their lot.

Be Steadfast"

But you man of God, go ahead and preach the truth without any compromise. It may be very painful that supposed members of the house are seeking to hand you over. There are times when even the same people you have been sent to bring out of captivity rise up against you because they have been made to believe a lie. Take the example of people who have been made to believe that the greater you give to the church, the more secured your salvation. Such people have no interest in holiness and would make money out of any means just to give to the church so God would love them more. Their joy is derived from this. And now when you come with the truth that God is not interested in their money, that in fact He wants their hearts and not their money, that all money given without first being in the right relationship with God is an abomination to Him, what do you expect from such people? A good welcome? Of course not, both they and their hirelings for shepherds will rise up against you. For the shepherd, you will be curbing their income. For the sheep, you will be taking away their refuge from sin. I believe that is why when *"The priests, the prophets and all the people heard Jeremiah speak these words in the house of the LORD. But as soon as Jeremiah finished telling all the people everything the LORD had commanded him to say, the priests, the prophets and all the people seized him and said, 'You must die!'"* (Jeremiah 26:7, 8)

Chapter 11: Hypocrites in the House

Yes death! That is the penalty for speaking the truth, for taking sides with the God the people have turned away from. Today we find Hananiahs in almost every area of ministry with their *"message from the Lord"* willing to oppose and destroy Jeremiahs and their ministry. It is a sad thing that supposed ministers would plot the fall of others; that they would rise up to propagate lies and slander others for the sole purpose of personal gain. But listen to what Jehovah says,

> *"25I have heard what the prophets say who prophesy lies in my name. They say, 'I had a dream! I had a dream!' 26 How long will this continue in the hearts of these lying prophets, who prophesy the delusions of their own minds? 27They think the dreams they tell one another will make my people forget my name, just as their fathers forgot my name through Baal worship. 28Let the prophet who has a dream tell his dream, but let the one who has my word speak it faithfully. For what has straw to do with grain?" declares the LORD. 29"Is not my word like fire," declares the LORD, "and like a hammer that breaks a rock in pieces? 30"Therefore," declares the LORD, "I am against the prophets who steal from one another words supposedly from me. 31Yes," declares the LORD, "I am against the prophets who wag their own tongues and yet declare, 'The LORD declares.' 32Indeed, I am against those who prophesy false dreams," declares the LORD. "They tell them and lead my people astray with their reckless lies, yet I did not send or appoint them. They do not benefit these people in the least," declares the LORD"* (Jeremiah 23:25-32).

O! That this generation would meditate on this book of Jeremiah so as to be enlightened. God says His word is like;

1. Fire
2. Hammer

Now tell me the work of fire and hammer. The word as fire is there to burn the chaff, to burn away the dross from the silver, to consume the darkness that fills the heart. Fire is very useful, yet very dangerous. The word as hammer is there to drive deep into the stony heart of man the truth of God and to break to pieces the barriers that have been built against God.

Now if the word you receive day after day, year after year leaves you unchanged, still comfortable with, and in your ungodliness, be sure that that is not the truth. This is what God is saying to you, *"Do not listen to what the prophets are prophesying to you; they fill you with false hopes. They speak visions from their own minds, not from the mouth of the LORD. They keep saying to those who despise me, 'The LORD says: You will have peace.' And to all who follow the stubbornness of their hearts they say, 'No harm will come to you.' But which of them has stood in the council of the LORD to see or to hear his word? Who has listened and heard his word?"* (Jeremiah 23:16-18)

How many are being filled with false hopes to make heaven? Millions! Peace and prosperity is being preached instead of repentance and holiness. The grace of God is magnified and His holiness rubbed in the mud. May the hound of heaven arise and vindicate His Name. For what does the Bible say?

> *"9 The coming of the lawless one will be in accordance with the work of Satan displayed in all kinds of counterfeit miracles, signs and wonders, 10 and in every sort of evil that deceives those who are perishing. They perish because they refused to love the truth and so be saved. 11 For this reason God sends them a powerful delusion so that they will believe the lie 12 and so that all will be condemned who have not believed the truth but have delighted in wickedness"* (2 Thessalonians 2:9-12).

A Cause to Despair?

> *"7 O LORD, you deceived me, and I was deceived; you overpowered me and prevailed. I am ridiculed all day long; everyone mocks me. 8 Whenever I speak, I cry out proclaiming violence and destruction. So the word of the LORD has brought me insult and reproach all day long. 9 But if I say, 'I will not mention him or speak any more in his name,' his word is in my heart like a fire, a fire shut up in my bones. I am weary of holding it in; indeed, I cannot. 10 I hear many whispering, 'Terror on every side! Report him! Let's*

Chapter 11: Hypocrites in the House

> *report him!' All my friends are waiting for me to slip, saying, 'Perhaps he will be deceived; then we will prevail over him and take our revenge on him' … ¹⁴cursed be the day I was born! May the day my mother bore me not be blessed! ¹⁵Cursed be the man who brought my father the news, who made him very glad, saying, 'A child is born to you—a son!' ¹⁶May that man be like the towns the LORD overthrew without pity. May he hear wailing in the morning, a battle cry at noon. ¹⁷For he did not kill me in the womb, with my mother as my grave, her womb enlarged forever. ¹⁸Why did I ever come out of the womb to see trouble and sorrow and to end my days in shame?" (Jeremiah 20:7-10, 14-18)*

The worst state for a minister to be in is a situation like this. Here we find Jeremiah in a flourishing ministry yet in despair - a man of God regretting having ever been born, cursing the one who took the good news of his birth to his father, cursing the day he was born. Is this where a minister should be? Now we all have seasons for *"lowness"* in our lives but when it reaches this level, it's a call for concern. What was the reason for such a state, more so for a man who had received assurance from God again and again and again and again. Does this not show how weak we are? That but for God's grace and strength we shall all abandon the race? Who is equal to such a task? If it had not been for the Lord, we all would have perished not from the hand of Satan but from discouragement and despair. Oft times, we find our trust and confidence dwindling under the pressure of persecution. If a minister finds himself in such a state, what about those he is called to lead, strengthen, and encourage?

What was the cause of this state of Jeremiah's

1. He was ridiculed all day long.
2. Everyone mocked him
3. The word of the Lord brought him insult
4. The word of the Lord brought him reproach all day long
5. All his friends waited for him to slip so as to prevail over him.
6. He heard whispering of terror for him
7. God had overpowered him and prevailed

8. The word was like fire in his bones when he attempted to keep it.

There are two basic lessons you and I can draw from here:

1. That unless there is death to the applause of men, death to fame and popularity, a day will come when all will be abandoned. That unless there is a total willingness to become unpopular if need be, to suffer shame, reproach, and rejection even from close friends and relatives, the battle is already lost. Is this not what the Savoir meant as carrying one's cross and following him? What does the cross bring but shame, reproach, rejection, and mockery? Everyone who carries the cross, carries it out of the city to a place where no selfish interest is realized.
2. That unless one is arrested, conquered and subdued by the Spirit of God, that unless God has taken hold of the whole person, in Jeremiah's, own words, *"unless God has overpowered and prevailed over"* an individual, that one will find himself running helter-skelter from the will of God in the face of pressure. May you take total hold of all that I am, Father, break my stubbornness and strong will, arrest and subdue me that I may be under Your influence at all times, everywhere and in everything. Do this for the sole sake of Your glory. That I may truly be useful in Your hands. Amen.

Chapter Twelve

A Renewed Trust

We thank God for His Spirit who is always there to comfort us and renew our hope and trust in the Father. I remember a few years ago in the university when I was one of the leaders of the students' work of our assembly. There were moments when one felt like giving up the whole thing. Results were not forthcoming and most of those who were supposed to be leading were not cooperating. However, few of them were available and one could count on them. During such low moments, you find yourself lifting up your eyes to the throne and receiving new strength and courage. At such a time in Jeremiah's life, we see him lifting up his eye again to the source of his strength and renewing his trust in God.

> *"But the LORD is with me like a mighty warrior; so my persecutors will stumble and not prevail. They will fail and be thoroughly disgraced; their dishonor will never be forgotten. O LORD Almighty, you who examine the righteous and probe the heart and mind, let me see your vengeance upon them, for to you I have committed my cause. Sing to the LORD! Give praise to the LORD! He rescues the life of the needy from the hands of the wicked"* (Jeremiah 20:11-13).

He saw anew that the Lord was with him just as He had promised. He saw that his persecutors would stumble and not prevail, that they will fail and be thoroughly disgraced, and that God rescues. If you and I too can learn to constantly lift our eyes up to the throne of grace, we shall always find new reasons to press on and new strength and courage to sustain us.

Going Where Duty Calls

> *"This is what the LORD says: 'Go down to the palace of the king of Judah and proclaim this message there:*
> *"This is what the LORD says: 'Stand in the courtyard of the LORD's house and speak to all the people of the towns of Judah who come to worship in the house of the LORD. Tell them everything I command you; do not omit a word'"'"* (Jeremiah 22:1, 26:2).

Many a time, the place where duty calls is always the place of danger. The man who ministers everywhere he is sent to has decided to face the danger associated to the place of duty. Here we find Jeremiah being sent to the very place were his life had earlier (at least once) been threatened. God at this time was saying to Jeremiah. *"I rescued you in past from the clutches of those who desired your life. You remain invincible as long as I am with you. Now rise and go to these places once more. And I will be with you as before."* The promise of God to you shall be put to the test by God Himself.

The things you have believed of Him shall come under test to prove the genuineness of your faith. He had promised to be with Jeremiah and to make him a fortified city. Though the people fought against him, they could not overcome him. Now you and I have been promised victory against our enemies. God has not said we shall not be attacked. They shall attack, they shall *"come sweeping like the flood"* but will never overcome us.

In this Christian life, the problem is not that storms come our way but, how we react to them. The problem is not that we meet dangers but how we brace ourselves in the face of dangers. Shall we trust our God and move on, proclaiming the victory of Christ even in places where the enemy has hoisted his flag of apparent victory? That place where it is forbidden to speak the Name of Jesus, shall we not brave ourselves up and speak His Name, come what may?

May God forgive me for not proclaiming Christ to my students, for not having mentioned His Name outrightly even after two weeks of teaching. At such a moment where duty calls and danger threatens, the man who shall discharge his duty is the one who has laid his life on the altar of God, the altar of the Gospel. Yeah! The one who will lose his life for His sake or the Gospel's and yet find it. All you and I need do is believe that the One who called us to such places will not leave us to ourselves. In this same light, David Brainerd prayed, *"Here I am, Lord. Send me, send me to the end of the earth; send me to the rough, the savage pagans of the wilderness; send me from all that is called comfort in earth, or earthly comfort; send me to death itself, if it be but in thy service and to promote the Kingdom"*. And if death should come, remember that; *"Death is a glorious event for one going to Jesus"* David Livingstone.

From Prison into a Cistern

> *"Jeremiah started to leave the city to go to the territory of Benjamin to get his share of the property among the people there. But when he reached the Benjamin Gate, the captain of the guard, whose name was Irijah son of Shelemiah, the son of Hananiah, arrested him and said, 'You are deserting to the Babylonians!' 'That's not true!' Jeremiah said. 'I am not deserting to the Babylonians.' But Irijah would not listen to him; instead, he arrested Jeremiah and brought him to the officials. They were angry with Jeremiah and had him beaten and imprisoned in the house of Jonathan the secretary, which they had made into a prison"* (Jeremiah 37:12-15).

> *"Then the officials said to the king, 'This man should be put to death. He is discouraging the soldiers who are left in this city, as well as all the people, by the things he is saying to them. This man is not seeking the good of these people but their ruin.' 'He is in your hands,' King Zedekiah answered. 'The king can do nothing to oppose you.' So they took Jeremiah and put him into the cistern of Malkijah, the king's son, which was in the courtyard of the guard. They lowered Jeremiah by ropes into the cistern; it had no water in it, only mud, and Jeremiah sank down into the mud"* (Jeremiah 38:4-6).

My heart goes out to the countless people who are now in jail for the sake of the gospel, those who have defiled the rules of men in order that the Kingdom of our Lord may prosper. Most are men and women whom many do not know but in their little corner they are braving it out in the storm and the flames of torture and imprisonment. Many of the martyrs are known only to the council of heaven and the little villages or towns where they were killed and their lives poured out as an offering before their God and Savior. Have you come across that book *"Tortured for His Faith"* by Halaran Porpov? Or "Tortured for Christ" by Richard Wundbrand? In these pages you will find the true story of those who suffered bitter agony in the hands of Satan for their faith and belief.

Unless a man had encountered God in a most transforming way, there was no way such a person could continue in the faith. For at such times, all those who played religion abandoned the way. As I read through *"Tortured for His Faith"*, I saw just how a minister could brave it out though he was apparently left alone. He went through what we find Jeremiah going through here; torture, imprisonment, and death (had not God rescued him).

I wish to encourage all those who are going through storms and flames of different magnitudes. You are facing what was and is still being faced by countless people professing Christ Jesus. Think of those in Muslim lands, in Buddhist and Hindu lands, and worst of all in communist lands. Think of them and thank God that there are others like yourself who are suffering because of the truth they proclaim in their messages.

Let's return to our narrative for a moment. At this time in Jeremiah's life, the King under whose rule his ministry began had been succeeded by two apostate Kings: Jehoiakim who defiantly burnt the scroll of the Lord's message and now his brother Zedekiah whom the Bible says, *"Neither he nor his attendants nor the people of the land paid any attention to the words the LORD had spoken through Jeremiah the prophet"* (Jeremiah 37:2).

It is but clear that when the ruler of a nation is righteous, that nation will be led into righteousness, the reverse is also true. King Zedekiah tried in private to corrupt Jeremiah who held on only to what God asked him to proclaim (vs 17). We do not know for how long Jeremiah stayed in prison but the Holy Spirit lets us know it was for a long time. After a long time in a dungeon, surely if given the opportunity to come out, unless you know the God who called you to His service, you shall accept your release at whatever terms.

How often do some act differently from what they preach and teach. Earlier Jeremiah had declared the portion of he who trusts in man, the one who depended on man. May be I take a review of those verses *"This is what the LORD says: 'Cursed is the one who trusts in man, who depends on flesh for his strength and whose heart turns away from the LORD. He will be like a bush in the wastelands; he will not see prosperity when it comes. He will dwell in the parched places of the desert, in a salt land where no one lives'"* (Jeremiah 17:5-6).

But had he not quickly turned to unrighteous Zedekiah for favor? Was he not now laying his petition before this unrighteous king? Listen to his pleas:

> *"But now, my lord the king, please listen. Let me bring my petition before you: Do not send me back to the house of Jonathan the secretary or I will die there"* (Jeremiah 37:20).

Hitting Rock Bottom

Well, King Zedekiah granted his request and transferred him from the dungeon to the courtyard where he was taken *"proper care"* of. But for how long did that freedom last? We shall see as we proceed. When Jeremiah continued to proclaim the word of God, he was again arrested this time not by a soldier but by the religious rulers of his time and sentenced to death. Before the execution, he was brought to the man who at first had seemingly granted him amnesty and these are his words: *"He is in your hands; the king can do nothing to oppose you"*. I can imagine the sweat which ran down Jeremiah's face, the one who once gave him confidence was now abandoning him to death. What lesson can we draw from here?

Surely man will always fail you. You cannot depend on man for your deliverance: all efforts you make to negotiate your *'release'* will only lead you to deeper trouble. Had Jeremiah remained in prison, surely God's deliverance could have come at the appropriate time. Now his attempt to work out his own deliverance got him into deeper troubles. Does that mean anything to you? Is God speaking to you? Will you wait for the Lord's deliverance? You better wait!

> *"So they took Jeremiah and put him into the cistern of Malkijah, the king's son, which was in the courtyard of the guard. They lowered Jeremiah by ropes into the cistern; it had no water in it, only mud, and Jeremiah sank down into the mud"* (Jeremiah 38:6).

I do not know what your haste has taken you into. But maybe you find yourself in a tight corner because you would not wait on the Lord. Maybe the enemy has lowered you into a waterless cistern with no rock for you to stand on and now you find yourself sinking down into the mud. Or maybe already you have sunk into the mud with no hope of coming out. For surely at this place, there was no way he could negotiate his own deliverance.

Is it not true that God will always bring us to a point of total surrender? A point where the help of man cannot be found and where even our own strength is useless? At such a point, Jeremiah's only hope was the Lord. If the Lord abandoned him, nothing awaited him but painful death, so now he was compelled to wait in a more humiliating circumstance. Surely, God will never share His glory with man.

Have you sunk because of the enemy? Your ministry seems to have ended, no hope of rising any longer. You seem to have hit rock bottom and you cannot sink any further? Where you are, there is nothing you can do but pray? For the only person available to hear your cry is the God of heaven. In the proceeding verses we see how God worked out Jeremiah's deliverance and he was lifted up out of the mud and restored to his ministry and God's promise to him had been fulfilled. You see Jeremiah was lifted out of the cistern and still confined, but God brought about his final deliverance through a pagan army commander.

The truth is that the Bible does not tell us in this case the glories which Jeremiah received in this life but I believe his labor was not in vain. God has in store for him rewards which are meant only for those who have stood the test of ministering against the tides and holding fast unwaveringly to the promises of God. We saw that he was not perfect but from his life we all can learn and correct or avoid our own mistakes.

I believe Jeremiah prayed something like this when God lifted him out of the mud

> *"I waited patiently for the LORD; he turned to me and heard my cry. He lifted me out of the slimy pit, out of the mud and mire; he set my feet on a rock and gave me a firm place to stand. He put a new song in my mouth, a hymn of praise to our God. Many will see and fear and put their trust in the LORD. Blessed is the man who makes the LORD his trust, who does not look to the proud, to those who turn aside to false gods. Many, O LORD my God, are the wonders you have done. The things you planned for us no one can recount to you; were I to speak and tell of them, they would be too many to declare"* (Psalm 40:1–5).

That is what God does for those who wait on Him. From the slimy pit and the mud and mire, He lifts them up and gives them a firm place to stand and declare His wonders and greatness. Glory to His Name!

Part Four

Lessons in the Storm
(Why Storms?)

Chapter Thirteen

A Call to Suffer

"Now if we are children, then we are heirs—heirs of God and co-heirs with Christ, if indeed we share in his sufferings in order that we may also share in his glory. I consider that our present sufferings are not worth comparing with the glory that will be revealed in us" (Romans 8:17-18).

Surely you are quite aware and maybe certain that we are co-heirs with Christ. I am sure this fact is indisputably written on the table of your heart in bold and this brings comfort to your soul. Surely you have the hope of sharing in the glory that will be the saints' when Christ shall return to earth in the splendor and majesty of His holiness. You have the hope, indisputably, of walking the golden streets of that city where God Himself will be light for His people. Too many Christians have this kind of awareness and surely there is every reason for it.

My concern is that too few of those aware of the glory side of it are aware of the suffering side of it. The call to share in the glory of Christ is a call to suffer. This is an indisputable truth; you cannot receive the glory without accepting the suffering. They are inseparable entities. For Christ to have been glorified He had to suffer and since no student is greater than his master we too have to suffer in order to be glorified along with Him who first suffered.

When shall we share in His glory? When we share in His suffering! Shunning suffering means shunning the glory that comes after it. Does this therefore mean that God's children should go about looking for ways through which they can suffer? Does It mean you and I have to watch for opportunities to suffer? Absolutely not! No child of God should go around creating *"scenes of suffering"* but we each must accept it as a part of the life to which we have been called. When the opportunities arise for you to suffer for His sake, do not run away from them. Accept them as means of identification with Him. Someone rightly said *"no cross no crown!"* Now, that is Christian truth. Do you want the crown? Then accept the cross.

Remember the Lord said *"if anyone should come after me, he must deny himself and take up his cross and follow me"* (Mark 8:34). Now what does the cross signify? Suffering, shame, disgrace, humiliation, and ultimately death for the sake of another, with no selfish gain in it. Christ carried His cross for us; all He did was for mankind, to bring us back to the glory once forfeited. Do you see that? He had no gain in carrying His cross. The process of carrying that cross to Golgotha brought Him nothing but pain and agony for your sake.

Now in carrying your own cross, it is for the sake of another, maybe a brother, a sister, a friend, or any loved one. Maybe for someone who means nothing to you or maybe your enemy. But ultimately you are called to suffer for the sake of Christ – the One who held nothing back to save you. He gave up His throne in all His glory and gave up His very life too. Would you hold back from such a person? Now taking up your cross is a must in the Christian life yet a voluntary act, Christ said of Himself;

> *"17The reason my Father loves me is that I lay down my life—only to take it up again. 18No one takes it from me, but I lay it down of my own accord. I have authority to lay it down and authority to take it up again. This command I received from my Father"* (John 10:17-18).

To save mankind He had to suffer but this was not a compulsion. He had authority to lay it down. In the same way, if we are to share in His glory we must carry our crosses and we should carry them voluntarily, not under compulsion. Has He called us to something He never went through? *"To this you were called, because Christ suffered for you, leaving you an example that you should follow in his steps"* (1 Peter 2:21).

Yeah to this you were called: to suffering for the sake of another, following the example of Christ and that of the heroes of Christian faith down through the ages. Let us stop to take a look at His perfect example in the school of suffering.

Jesus' Example

> *"And he said, 'The Son of Man must suffer many things and be rejected by the elders, chief priests and teachers of the law, and he must be killed and on the third day be raised to life'" (Luke 9:22).*

> *"For the Son of Man in his day will be like the lightning, which flashes and lights up the sky from one end to the other. But first he must suffer many things and be rejected by this generation" (Luke 17:24-25).*

> *"Did not the Christ have to suffer these things and then enter his glory?" (Luke 24:46)*

Jesus knew that He had to suffer. To Him it was a must and He was totally aware of it. He made provision for it throughout His life on earth. He was never taken by surprise when suffering came, for He Himself had declared it. When betrayed, He endured it. When rejected by the religious authorities, He accepted it. He never tried to lose His identity or to compromise His vision for the sake of *"peace"* or comfort. Even when disowned by he who claimed to be His closest companion, He never took offence. What can we learn from His examples? What is it the Spirit of God must write in bold across your heart? That though the Christian life is a glorious one, with it there is suffering, rejection, and ultimately death, yes even daily death. Those are the footsteps in which you should walk.

Suffering for the Lord

> *"The apostles left the Sanhedrin, rejoicing because they had been counted worthy of suffering disgrace for the Name"* (Acts 5:41).

> *"I'll show him how much he must suffer for my name"* (Acts 9:16).

Like the apostles, you and I should count ourselves worthy of suffering for His Name's sake. This can be in several ways:

Persecution from those who oppose your faith in Christ; it can be that you are suffering financial difficulties because you have refused for the sake of Christ to soil your hands in one way or another. Maybe you are allowing yourself to be cheated. May be others are taking advantage of your faith and there is nothing you can do about it. Rejoice and count yourself worthy of suffering disgrace for His Name. If you were not a professing Christian such suffering won't ever come your way. Be happy that it is for His Name's sake.

Now, of the greatest missionary of all times, the Lord said *"I will show him what he must suffer for My Name"*. The truth is that God has called some of us to a life of suffering. Suffering for His Name sake. Now look at a brief description of Paul's life in Acts and what he himself testifies in his epistles. His life was void of suffering as a successful young man in his days enjoying the climb on the staircase of worldly success. His suffering began when he became a Christian.

It was clear to him that he had to suffer and that he was called for that. So he endured it with all joy. He said of himself, *"And now, compelled by the Spirit, I am going to Jerusalem, not knowing what will happen to me there. I only know that in every city the Holy Spirit warns me that prison and hardships are facing me. However, I consider my life worth nothing to me, if only I may finish the race and complete the task the Lord Jesus has given me—the task of testifying to the gospel of God's grace"* (Acts 20:22-24). He was aware and lived in consciousness of the fact that he had been promised suffering and hardship everywhere he went.

There is some kind of gospel that goes out today inviting people to a Christian life void of pain, trouble or disgrace. A Christian life that brings an end to all problems. A gospel which regards suffering as an enemy to the Christian. These evangelists forget that without Christ, some of them lived a happy life and trouble began when the lips pledged allegiance to Christ. Shameful ways of making money and living in comfort have to go and Christian integrity embraced to the core of it. Many of such people are untrained in any noble vocation. What awaits such a man but intense suffering at least for some time before he is helped? Some are fired from their jobs when they become Christians.

When people are promised a life void of suffering, it is no doubt if they turn away and abandon the Lord in times of intense trials and testing. They are often willing to sell out for anything that would bring them comfort. For they think it strange that they suffer. The whole truth must be preached and if need be, suffering promised and let those who are willing to carry their cross follow Him.

Unlike the devil who shows you glittering things but intense suffering behind them, God in most cases gives you the glory behind suffering. This difference, when understood will bring a lot of changes to many a life that appears miserable because of a misconception of Christian doctrine.

More than Just Believing

> *"For it has been granted to you on behalf of Christ not only to believe on him, but also to suffer for him, since you are going through the same struggle you saw I had, and now hear that I still have"* (Philippians 1:29-30).

I like that word *"granted"*. Suffering to Christians is a grant and not a misfortune. There is something greater than just believing in Christ. This is the basis but yet there is something more to it which you must receive with gratitude, a grant from your Father – suffering for Christ. O! That God will open our eyes to behold this truth and our minds to accept it. For the Christian, suffering is a grant. Have you believed that, that suffering is indeed a grant? That you would believe it with all your heart and with every ounce of your energy! As such, what should you do? Now that you have understood this truth, is there anything you can do? Yes there is, it seems very trivial yet much depends on it. It is that you should:

Expect Suffering

> "We sent Timothy, who is our brother and God's fellow worker in spreading the gospel of Christ, to strengthen and encourage you in your faith, so that no one would be unsettled by these trials. You know quite well that we were destined for them. In fact, when we were with you, we kept telling you that we would be persecuted. And it turned out that way, as you well know" (1 Thessalonians 3:2-4).

> "[10]You, however, know all about my teaching, my way of life, my purpose, faith, patience, love, endurance, [11]persecutions, sufferings—what kinds of things happened to me in Antioch, Iconium and Lystra, the persecutions I endured. Yet the Lord rescued me from all of them. [12]In fact, everyone who wants to live a godly life in Christ Jesus will be persecuted" (2 Timothy 3:10-12).

> "If the world hates you, keep in mind that it hated me first. If you belonged to the world, it would love you as its own. As it is, you do not belong to the world, but I have chosen you out of the world. That is why the world hates you. Remember the words I spoke to you: 'No servant is greater than his master.' If they persecuted me, they will persecute you also. If they obeyed my teaching, they will obey yours also. They will treat you this way because of my name, for they do not know the One who sent me" (John. 15:18-21).

The list of passages could go on and on. Why did Paul and his companion send Timothy? That he may strengthen and encourage the believers in Thessalonica, telling them that trials and difficulties should bring no uncertainty in the mind of a believer. We are destined for them. Do you see that? To Christians suffering is a means to destiny. Trials must come, and you cannot change that, for you will dive out of tune with true Christianity. Just as God predestined you for salvation, so you are destined for trials. There is not one without the other. Thus, as a Christian you should expect suffering as part of your life.

Chapter 13: A Call to Suffer

To Timothy, Paul said *"in fact, everyone who wants to live a godly life in Christ must be persecuted"*, in other words, must suffer and must face trials and difficulties. He encouraged him from his own experience. May you and I have such experience, more of them that we too may encourage others to brave it out when faced with difficulties. Now let us turn to our Lord's teaching on this, on that eve of his death and in His very first sermon:

> *"If the world hates you, keep in mind that it hated me first. If you belonged to the world, it would love you as its own. As it is, you do not belong to the world, but I have chosen you out of the world. That is why the world hates you. Remember the words I spoke to you: 'No servant is greater than his master. If they persecuted me, they will persecute you also. If they obeyed my teaching, they will obey yours also. They will treat you this way because of my name, for they do not know the One who sent me"* (John. 15:18-21).

> *"Blessed are those who are persecuted because of righteousness, for theirs is the kingdom of heaven. "Blessed are you when people insult you, persecute you and falsely say all kinds of evil against you because of me. Rejoice and be glad, because great is your reward in heaven, for in the same way they persecuted the prophets who were before you"* (Matthew 5:10-12).

Our Lord taught that, it is a blessing to suffer for righteousness sake. That it is a blessing when insulted for His Name sake, when accusing fingers are pointed at you because of your commitment to Christ. Instead of being filled with sadness or shame, He tells you to rejoice and be glad. Why? Because great is your reward in heaven. Not just an ordinary reward but a great reward, great in every sense of the word. Thus, in His very first sermon our Lord emphasized on the importance and blessedness of suffering for His sake. At the very beginning, He let them understand that it won't all be a bed of roses but that they should prepare to face the trials.

Anything that the world does to you should not be considered strange. It did the same to your Lord. In other words at His last sermon, teaching His inner circle, He gave them the reason why they would suffer.

Introducing Himself in the book of revelation, this is what Apostle John wrote.

> *"I, John, your brother and companion in the suffering and kingdom and patient endurance that are ours in Jesus, was on the island of Patmos because of the word of God and the testimony of Jesus"* (Revelation 1:9).

He was a brother first of all which, therefore, made him a companion in
1. The suffering.
2. The Kingdom.
3. Patient endurance,

that are ours in Christ Jesus. The first identity He gave was not the Kingdom, in this sense the glory of belonging to Christ, but the suffering that is in Christ Jesus. He was in fact saying he couldn't make claim to the Kingdom without first making claim to the suffering. Many people will want to identify themselves as partners in the Kingdom but not partners in the suffering. So though we suffer, the fact that we share in the glories of the Kingdom should cause us to patiently endure when all else is calling us to give up.

An Invitation

Paul had gotten a profound revelation about the glories of suffering for Christ and so he wouldn't keep to himself. He had received so much of the grant and saw how great his reward would be that he invited others to share in his suffering.

> *"So do not be ashamed to testify about our Lord, or ashamed of me his prisoner. But join with me in suffering for the gospel, by the power of God"*
> (2 Timothy 1:8).

Paul was actually in simple terms inviting Timothy to share in this privilege that is ours in Christ like any other. Someone has discovered gold and is inviting you to share in it, to come and gather as much of it as you want. Won't you joyfully and hastily respond? Now, is not Paul calling us to gather jewels for ourselves in heaven by being part of the suffering here on earth? How can you dare live in all the luxury now and amass just hay and stubble for eternity? May God open your eyes and may you make haste to this glorious invitation of all times, second only to the invitation of Jesus to all the thirsty and hungry to come drink and eat of Him.

Before we go on to give the reasons why we must face storms, let us see how we can avoid unnecessary storms, storms that will bring us no reward. For though every storm has something to teach us, some have no glory to bring us.

Chapter Fourteen

Avoiding Unnecessary Storms

"It is better, if it is God's will, to suffer for doing good than for doing evil." (1 Peter 3:17).

Now this verse makes us to know that there are sufferings which may befall us that are not God's will for us. If it is God's will, we should gladly accept it but if it results from sin or rebellion, avoid it altogether for it shall bring no glory. God's will is that we should suffer for doing good, not as a result of rebellion. Now let us look at two instances where some group of people in the Bible faced storms, which could altogether have been avoided.

The Disciples in an Avoidable Storm

"When evening came, his disciples went down to the lake, where they got into a boat and set off across the lake for Capernaum. By now it was dark, and Jesus had not yet joined them. A strong wind was blowing and the waters grew rough. When they had rowed three or three and a half miles, they saw Jesus approaching the boat, walking on the water; and they were terrified. But he said to them, "It is I; don't be afraid." Then they were willing to take him into the boat, and immediately the boat reached the shore where they were heading" (John 6:16-21).

Here we see the disciples going down to the lake without the Lord present. From going to a lake without the Savior, they boarded a boat without Him and the result was a storm. Often, the danger is that when one move without the Savior is made successfully, it is very difficult to restrain from the second, which may result in a catastrophe. The flash point can easily be attained in such situations. More on that later!

The first lesson we learn here is that as Christians, there is absolute danger in advancing without the assurance that the Savior is present. It is absolutely necessary to sit and wait and tarry and delay in all things so that the Lord joins, before take-off by giving His approval. Until Jesus is present, there is no light. Sailing in whatever direction is sailing in darkness. In your relationships, plans, projects, without the security of the Savior's presence, make no advancement. Yet many of us dare to make a sail without the Savior, we lead our lives without Him.

For how long have you sailed in darkness? In darkness the storms grow tougher and rougher. There is no hope in darkness. Any sail without the Savior's presence is to sail deeper into trouble. What appears to be a little pleasure trip may turn out to cost you a lifetime. May I repeat that to sail without His presence is to sail in the dark. And any sail in the dark is bound to meet storms. Before the disciples met the Savior, remember they were fishermen; they had been used to sailing without Him. So they thought it altogether the same - now that they had pledged allegiance to Him-to sail without Him. Now there is real danger in acting out of experience from your life as an unbeliever, for that will be presumption.

Before, you were the lord of your own life, now there is a new LORD, the King of the universe. When such a sail is made, the Lord will allow you to go a considerable distance in the storm before He comes to your rescue. He will always come when you are in danger. I want to say that the Lord is always approaching the storm tossed boats of His children but do they see Him? Do you see Him approaching yours? When you see Him do you recognize Him? In a storm it is very difficult to distinguish and sense the presence of the Lord. It is difficult to recognize the moves of God at such moments and thus it will take God a miracle (it took Jesus in this case walking on water) to approach your far-assailed storm-and-wind- tossed boat. Yeah a miracle to rescue you; and until you recognize His manifestation you will not recognize Him. And until you recognize Him, you will not take Him in, and you must be willing to take Him in for Him to come in. You must invite Him in before He can enter.

He said, *"My sheep know my voice"*. It is absolutely necessary to know the Savior's voice such that even when you cannot recognize His presence you will be able to recognize His *"it is I; do not be afraid"*. As you take Him in, His presence will make the difference no matter the darkness and intensity of the storm. No matter how rough and tough the sail has been, no matter how far the sail has gone, the Lord wants to come in; He wants to join the sail and make the difference. There has been no hope of reaching the other side of the shore, so He wants to come in and offer a new hope to your hopeless or near hopeless situation. But are you willing to take Him in?

In every stormy sail, there reaches a point of no return to the place of departure. It may be the first, second, or third step. You will never know it and after that point if God must intervene, then it is not to rescue but to help you face the storm in His power. It is to help you cross to the other side of the shore where you were heading. In life's storms and wind, our Savior, I believe has three options.

1. To calm the storm, or
2. To lift you out of it, or
3. To help you face the storm.

The choice is His but He will always act out of His infinite love, knowledge, wisdom and holiness. Yeah! He takes all that into consideration. His love moves him to intervene. His knowledge leads Him to choose what to do. His wisdom enables Him to manage the situation and produce the best out of the storm. His holiness causes Him to act justly and do nothing that will later profane His Name.

Now, where are you sailing to without the Lord? Return to Him where you left Him before it is too late. Do not take another step without Him for that maybe your fatal crossing. For example you might get into a relationship without the Lord's approval and get into marriage. At that point as Christians there is no return, He can only help you endure and face the storm that will result. So decide that,

1. You will start no relationship without the Savior's approval.
2. You will get into no vocation without the Savior.
3. You will make no journey without the Savior making it with you.
4. You will not invest in any business without Him investing.
5. You will not be involved in any project without Him committing Himself to it.
6. You will not involve in any battle without Him leading.
7. You will not involve in any conversation without Him being a part of it.

An Avoidable Storm – II

Now turn to your Bible and read the narrative from where we shall draw our inspiration at this time. Turn to Acts 27 and read through that chapter. Then follow through as we examine in details this passage of scripture.

> *"Much time had been lost, and sailing had already become dangerous because by now it was after the Fast. So Paul warned them, "Men, I can see that our voyage is going to be disastrous and bring great loss to ship and cargo, and to our own lives also." But the centurion, instead of listening to what Paul said, followed the advice of the pilot and of the owner of the ship. Since the harbor was unsuitable to winter in, the majority decided that we should sail on, hoping to reach Phoenix and winter there. This was a harbor in Crete, facing both southwest and northwest"* (Acts 9: 9-12).

Often, you would acknowledge, time appears to run too fast, as one always seems like he is far behind in accomplishing his goals and dreams. We live in a generation where time flies just too quickly and everyone struggles to catch

Chapter 14: Avoiding Unnecessary Storms

up with it. Thus, because we must *"catch"* up with time, little or no precaution is taken in the kind of things one gets engaged in. Seldom do we wait or heed the instructions of spiritual authority. Because of time, many who have sensed danger have persisted in their own ways and many a life has been shipwrecked in an attempt *"to meet up"*. From every indication, there was danger to continue sail, and it was still dangerous harboring. Paul warned of eminent destruction should the voyage continue. But the majority decided that it was more dangerous harboring there.

Is your life ruled by popular opinion? Do you listen to the counsel of spiritual men and women God has placed over you? I am quite sure the people in the ship considered Paul as just an ordinary prisoner and despised his advice though many of them knew for sure that he was a man of God. The person whom God may use to prevent you from a dangerous sail may have no worldly wisdom. In the eyes of the world, he or she may be nothing, but yet God has decided to speak through him. How do you take the counsel of your authorities? You may have very genuine reasons to persist in the course you are taking but would you seek counsel and heed to it?

Maybe the advice the man of God will give you would appear totally contrary to that of experts of the world, for what experience had Paul in sailing compared to the pilot or owner of the ship? What did he know about the interpretation of weather conditions in the course of sailing? Was it not all together foolish that he should be advising the people in their own field?

Maybe you are an expert in what you are about to do and there is every indication, at least, according to worldly wisdom to proceed. The majority of the people around you deem it necessary that you proceed and they have cast their votes in your favor. I advise you as a Christian, to seek godly counsel, or better still heed the counsel that has been given by the spiritual authority. He may stand alone in his counsel, but heed to it. My heart goes out to many a congregation which has been shipwrecked as a result of some majority vote of its *"board of directors"* – no doubt the Holy Spirit who is really supposed to direct the affairs of the Church has been kept aside. He has been overthrown from office and decisions of the fate of many lie in the hands of a few in *"the board of directors"*.

Have Christian sittings become parliaments were bills are passed? Is not heaven supposed to govern the affairs of a Church? But often heaven is kept aside and man brought to the position of having the final say. Let us return to the Holy Spirit, if not, eminent destruction and derailment awaits many a ministry. It is time we return to *"thus says the Lord"*. If the *"board of directors"* is taking a decision it should be that for which God has been prayerfully sought. Do not hurry to catch up with time for you might end up losing all you have so worked for and even your own life or the future of that ministry? Maybe you care little about your own life but what about those that decision of yours is going to affect? Do you care about them? Have you taken into consideration what might befall them? I advise you to in every wise do.

The storm behind the breeze

> *"When a gentle south wind began to blow, they thought they had obtained what they wanted; so they weighed anchor and sailed along the shore of Crete. Before very long, a wind of hurricane force, called the "northeaster," swept down from the island. The ship was caught by the storm and could not head into the wind; so we gave way to it and were driven along.*
> *We took such a violent battering from the storm that the next day they began to throw the cargo overboard. On the third day, they threw the ship's tackle overboard with their own hands. When neither sun nor stars appeared for many days and the storm continued raging, we finally gave up all hope of being saved"* (VV 13-15, 18-20).

Do circumstances and favorable conditions dictate your decisions? The *"weather"* surrounding the atmosphere in which you have to take a decision seems quite favorable. Everything seems to be in your favor but have you sought God's opinion or that of His anointed? Do not allow circumstances to rule your life no matter how favorable they may appear, if not you are heading for a shipwreck. How favorable were the conditions when the people decided to sail, to move in the direction of the gentle south wind?

My friend, do not allow your life in any way to be driven by *"gentle south winds"* for what seems quite favorable may turn out against you before long.

In fact one could entitle this section *"The breeze that became a storm"*. *"Before very long a wind of hurricane force called the north-easter, swept down from the Island"*. The favorable *"south-easter"* breeze had become a disastrous *"north-easter"* hurricane before very long. Circumstances always change so one should not rely on them. The only sure thing is the word of the Lord to you. Do not forsake that. As a child of God you cannot do without it. The heathen may *"succeed"* without it but do not copy their examples.

Have you followed a gentle breeze and now before long your ship is caught in a violent storm? You can no longer head into the storm and you have decided to give in to it and so you are tossed to and fro by the wind in the storm. The pain is immense and you are hardly able to make the lifeboat secure. For now, it has gone out of your control. Disaster is eminent and can no longer be avoided. Have you begun experiencing the loss that could be avoided? Has the storm been so violent that you are now throwing the things you once valued and held in adorable esteem?

For many days or months or years, you have been badly battered by that single decision you took and yet no signs of relieve appear in the horizon. Neither the sun nor the stars have appeared for all this time. The storm has continued raging persistently and finally you have given up all hope of being saved? All hope is not gone, that is the good news. Jesus Christ is in control; He can come in and make the difference. Oh! That you may lift up your eyes to the throne of grace and find courage.

May your eyes be opened to see the angel whom God, out of mercy, has sent to bring you a message of hope and deliverance! May your ears be opened to hear His comforting voice of hope, *"do not be afraid"*. All material things may have been lost but God has decided to spare your life and to keep you spiritually alive.

If you continue the narrative, you will realize all but the lives of those in the ship was lost. The ship itself was completely destroyed but they all arrived safe on shore. Even now in your storm, if you *"take sounding"* you will realize there are signs of your deliverance. Your God is in the horizon, bringing to you His salvation so full and free, though not for your sake but His own Name's sake, for you merit nothing but a continuous battering from the raging storm.

Chapter Fifteen

Reasons for the Storms

Storms are not just some purposeless misfortunes which come our way; God allows them for some reasons as we will see below:

To Be Made Strong, Firm and Steadfast

> *"And the God of all grace, who called you to his eternal glory in Christ, after you have suffered a little while, will himself restore you and make you strong, firm and steadfast"* (1 Peter 5:10).

If you read through 1 Peter you will quickly notice that Peter was writing to a troubled people, who in diverse ways were going through the storms of life. First of all in the verse quoted above, he drew their attention to the glory they had been called to and spoke to them about the faithfulness of God. And this should be our attitude in stormy moments. Look up to the glory that awaits you if you go through. Think about the goodness and faithfulness of God who shall restore you after you have suffered a little while. Why only after you have suffered a little while? Because after the suffering you shall be made

1. Strong
2. Firm
3. Steadfast

- Strong to face future difficult moments. For each storm makes you strong and fortified to run the race to which you have been called.
- Firm because many a time, we are not firm on our faith, in the course we run. Storms come to make us firm. For in times of storms we quickly ensure our anchor holds on Christ the solid Rock and thus we are made firmer in our faith and belief.
- Steadfast because often in times of suffering, it becomes clear that certain possibilities are completely ruled out. Thus in a case where someone was wavering between many opinions, storms may come to bring him to focus and cause him to be steadfast and single minded.

Storms Are Lessons

"Although he was a son, he learned obedience from what he suffered" (Hebrews 5:8).

This talks of Christ, that He learned obedience through what He suffered. If you and I pay attention to the lessons the storms come along with, we shall readily accept them. For the things they teach us can be learned in no other way. You and I are often too stubborn and rebellious that we can only learn obedience through suffering. We can only learn to align ourselves with the will of God after going through storms. So storms are necessary because through them you learn obedience to God and are turned around from rebellion and hence from perdition, to the ways of obedience and salvation.

I am sure you can bear testimony to this from your own experience that storms come to teach you. David said, *"Before I was afflicted I went astray, but now I obey your word"* (Psalm 119:67).

Before affliction and suffering there is the tendency to stray from the right way but after affliction, obedience is formed in the inner man. He said again *"It was good for me to be afflicted so that I might learn your decrees"* (Psalm 119:71).

Afflictions make us learn Biblical truths. They bring us to learn more about the things of God. Yeah, More about His decrees that we could otherwise not have learnt!

For Perfection

> *"In bringing many sons to glory, it was fitting that God, for whom and through whom everything exists, should make the author of their salvation perfect through suffering"* (Hebrews 2:10).

If the most perfect Man who ever lived could be made perfect through suffering (And I say it with much reverence), what about you and I with our lot and lots of imperfections? Do you think there is any other way through which we too can be made perfect? Sufferings are like tools in the hands of the potter and pruning hooks in the hands of the vine dresser. He uses them to trim and smoothen our rough edges. He uses them to prune the wild branches that would otherwise prevent us from yielding good returns.

You see, often palm trees are pruned in preparation for future seasons so that they can produce good fruits and yield a good return. That is just the same thing with us. God uses suffering or trials to make us fruitful in Christian service. Have you seen a man who has gone through difficult times? Such a person comes out with much wisdom, godliness, and maturity. Periods of testing are periods of divine transformation. Thus suffering is necessary for your perfection.

Storms Are Messengers of God

> *"He makes winds his messengers, flames of fire his servants"* (Psalm 104:4).

How true it is that God makes winds His messengers and flames of fire His servants! Have you read of the east wind throughout the Bible? It is one of God's most faithful servants. Eliphaz said, *"for God does speak – now one way, now another – though man may not perceive it"* (Job 33:14). When certain things begin to happen to us, the question that must be asked is *"what message have these flames or storms brought?"*

An instance where God used storms to send across His message is the popular story of Jonah fleeing from God:

> *"The word of the LORD came to Jonah son of Amittai: "Go to the great city of Nineveh and preach against it, because its wickedness has come up before me." But Jonah ran away from the LORD and headed for Tarshish. He went down to Joppa, where he found a ship bound for that port. After paying the fare, he went aboard and sailed for Tarshish to flee from the LORD. Then the LORD sent a great wind on the sea, and such a violent storm arose that the ship threatened to break up. All the sailors were afraid and each cried out to his own god. And they threw the cargo into the sea to lighten the ship. But Jonah had gone below deck, where he lay down and fell into a deep sleep"* (Jonah 1:1-5).

Here is a prophet whom God sent on an assignment but who decided to go his own way. He thought he could run away from God, not knowing that God is everywhere. Knowing that God is everywhere, David said,

> *"Where can I go from your Spirit? Where can I flee from your presence? If I go up to the heavens, you are there; if I make my bed in the depths, you are there. If I rise on the wings of the dawn, if I settle on the far side of the sea, even there your hand will guide me, your right hand will hold me fast. If I say, "Surely the darkness will hide me and the light become night around me," even the darkness will not be dark to you; the night will shine like the day, for darkness is as light to you"* (Psalm 139:7-12).

There is no hiding place from the God of heaven. No matter how much a man tries to run from God, God will always use storms to bring him to his knees, a point of total surrender to the will of God. So this prophet in his strong self-will became blind to the truth he knew. For surely such a man should know that no one could escape from the Lord. Do you see what self-will can do? When one begins to run away from God, when one begins to fight with God, his vision becomes impaired and thus he becomes blind to truth he once knew. That is the truth and that counts for the derailment of many a minister today who once knew and preached truth but is now preaching first class heresy. It all can be traced to a point where the will of God was abandoned and the way of rebellion chosen. May this be a warning to all ministers and will-be ministers of the Word!

> *"Then the LORD sent a great wind on the sea, and such a violent storm arose that the ship threatened to break up"* (Jonah 1:4).

The storm of the Lord will oppose any sail that is against the will of God. God will not allow His chosen ones to escape from His will. Storms are at times warnings from the Lord that one is heading the wrong direction and the wise man will sit and ask himself what has gone wrong. And if you listen carefully, His hand will surely point to something in your life, which displeases Him. Something He does not want you to engage in but you stubbornly want to. In the narrative, the storm brought a message of the presence of an unwanted element in the ship, one who for no reason should be sailing for Tarshish.

The sailors understood this after throwing out the cargo to lighten the ship to no avail. They concluded that someone was surely responsible for that calamity. My brother, my sister, can it be that the storms you are facing are a result of an unwanted presence in your life? Can it be that there is something you must separate yourself from? You had better find out, prayerfully, what is responsible for your calamity. If not, no matter how much you pray for the storms to cease, they shall persist.

Maybe you have cried out to God for too long but there has been apparently no response. Begin to check your life, your engagements, or commitments. They are probably in the wrong direction. When lots were cast, it fell on Jonah. If you seek to know what is responsible for your storms, man, God will show you and you shall know. Can you imagine that even when they found out that Jonah was responsible for the storms and that the only solution was to throw him away the Bible says, *"Instead, the men did their best to row back to land. But they could not, for the sea grew even wilder than before."* (Jonah 1:13)?

People always try their best to keep what God does not want. They do everything to preserve that foreign body in their lives that God would rather it be destroyed. Yet increasingly the storms grow rougher and tougher and wilder before them. They fail to see that they cannot succeed in the battle against God. Do you know that which is responsible for the storms in your life? Will you throw it away? You may throw every other thing away but that won't bring the solution. Instead of throwing away Jonah, the sailors threw away the cargo as though it was responsible. There should be no attempt whatsoever to protect that which God is against, for this will only be a call for persistent storms.

> *"Then they took Jonah and threw him overboard, and the raging sea grew calm. At this the men greatly feared the LORD, and they offered a sacrifice to the LORD and made vows to him"* (Jonah 1:15-16).

Thank God after their unsuccessful attempt to preserve Jonah, they finally decided to throw him away. Maybe you too have a Jonah in your boat that you are trying to preserve. May you come to your senses and throw it away soonest. The result is that the storms in your life will subside for they must have sent across their message. God's messengers do not return to Him unless they have accomplished His purpose.

After this storm in Jonah's life, we find him in a tight corner deciding to go to Nineveh, the place he was supposed to go. May the storm of God turn you from your Tarshish to God's Nineveh and may you like Jonah obey and go to where the Lord is sending you. If not be prepared to be swallowed by your own fish. I don't know what that may be but God knows His methods.

Storms Come To Refine.

> *"See, I have refined you, though not as silver; I have tested you in the furnace of affliction"* (Isaiah 48:10).

God has placed much gold in us, but due to the fall it contains lots and lots of impurities. God as the goldsmith cannot use us effectively until we have been refined. The Bible says "Remove the dross from the silver, and out comes material for the silversmith". God is the silversmith or goldsmith but the dross in the gold is an obstacle to Him. So in order to refine, He passes us through the furnace of affliction. Man, the furnace is not a comfortable place to be but it produces things of great worth, value, and durability.

The things which sell high are those which have gone through a refining process. Take for example crude oil. It is bought cheap but after refining it becomes expensive. The furnace of affliction also comes to test a man's works. Remember that all we do here on earth shall be tested with fire. If it stands the test of fire, it shall be counted worthy of reward. If not, there shall be no reward. Accept the flames now so you shall not continue to build with hay and stubble. Let the flames burn away the hay and the stubble so that your works may rest on gold and precious stones.

Storms bring a new purpose

> "*Therefore, since Christ suffered in his body, arm yourselves also with the same attitude, because he who has suffered in his body is done with sin. As a result, he does not live the rest of his earthly life for evil human desires, but rather for the will of God*" (1 Peter 4:1-2).

> "*Dear friends, do not be surprised at the painful trial you are suffering, as though something strange were happening to you. But rejoice that you participate in the sufferings of Christ, so that you may be overjoyed when his glory is revealed. If you are insulted because of the name of Christ, you are blessed, for the Spirit of glory and of God rests on you. If you suffer, it should not be as a murderer or thief or any other kind of criminal, or even as a meddler. However, if you suffer as a Christian, do not be ashamed, but praise God that you bear that name*" (1Peter 4: 12-16).

My focus here is the connection between verses one and two. Without verse one, verse two is meaningless. The fact that one would not live his life for selfish human reasons as Christians, depends on the fact that you pass through suffering. In life, trials come to give you a new purpose and direction. They come to draw your attention to the fact that "*… none of us lives to himself* *alone and none of us dies to himself alone. ⁸If we live, we live to the Lord; and if we die, we die to the Lord. So, whether we live or die, we belong to the Lord."* (Romans 14:7-8).

A man who has suffered in his body dreads nothing and sees the urgent need to live henceforth for God. The man who suffers intensely becomes dead, totally dead to the appeals, offers, fame, and glories of the world. His one focus is to live for God and please Him. Most people who live in total surrender to God owe it to suffering and trials that came their way. So accept suffering as coming to give you a new purpose, to carry you to a higher place in your obedience and therefore fellowship with the Father, Son, and Holy Spirit.

Storms Are Proofs of God's Faithfulness

"I know, O LORD, that your laws are righteous, and in faithfulness you have afflicted me" (Psalms 119:75).

You know, many a time, you might be tempted to live as though you were self-sufficient. That you could take care of your every need, that you actually need no special intervention from God. And so your life seems to move smoothly without God. Remember how Jesus stood outside the self-sufficient church knocking that He be let in?

"You say, 'I am rich; I have acquired wealth and do not need a thing.' But you do not realize that you are wretched, pitiful, poor, blind and naked. 18I counsel you to buy from me gold refined in the fire, so you can become rich; and white clothes to wear, so you can cover your shameful nakedness; and salve to put on your eyes, so you can see. Here I am! I stand at the door and knock. If anyone hears my voice and opens the door, I will come in and eat with him, and he with me" (Revelation 3:17-18, 20).

Yeah He stands and knocks and one of the means through which He knocks at your door is through the storms. He is too faithful to allow His children to miss the blessedness of a life that totally depends on Him, a life that He is a full part of, where He dines and wines with the owner of that house. So storms come as a result of God's faithfulness to remind you of how pitiful, poor, blind, naked, shameful your life can be without Him. So indeed you may open wide the door of your heart.

This brings to mind a sketch that was presented by the Drama group of our local church: It was a young man who owned a house. After a persistent knock he finally let Christ into his house. But he took Him to the toilet and asked Him to stay just there. And the gentle Jesus in the sketch stayed just where He was asked to. Then came the devil, tormenting the life of that young man. When he cried and ran to Jesus, he asked Him why He did not intervene. Jesus wiped the tears from his cheeks and told him *"because you gave me just the key to your toilet"*. So the young man decided to hand Him the key to the kitchen this time.

The same scene kept on repeating, Satan kept on tormenting his life until he handed over the keys of every corner of his house to Jesus. And now, when the devil came again and knocked, the young man was about going to open the door, but since Jesus had the keys, He called him back and went to answer the knock Himself. Guess what, Satan fell on his knees begging for pardon that he had knocked on the wrong door.

When Jesus became Lord and Master of that house the torments from Satan were over. The storms had brought the young man to the point of handing over all to the Master's control. Now, that is just the Christian experience. Storms bring you to the point of total surrender. When God allows Satan to torment a life, it is part of His faithfulness to the individual concerned.

Through Storms God Reveals His Glory to Mankind

To better explain this point, let's look at the life of a young man who stood for His God in the face of persecution from a heathen King. This hero called Daniel was a young Hebrew on exile in Babylon.

Read Daniel 3. Here Daniel's friends are faced with the death treats because they will not bow down to an idol. The king decides that they be thrown into a blazing furnace seven times hotter. I like that number seven. Now, seven in the scripture is the number of perfection. And the seven times hotter furnace represents the epitome, the climax of the flames they were facing. But while in the flames they were not consumed. Rather, a fourth person had joined them and that was no other than the King of glory Himself. Amazed to see that they were not consumed, the king concluded that the God of these men is the true God. This is what the pagan King proclaimed:.

> 'Then Nebuchadnezzar said, "Praise be to the God of Shadrach, Meshach and Abednego, who has sent his angel and rescued his servants! They trusted in him and defied the king's command and were willing to give up their lives rather than serve or worship any god except their own God. Therefore I decree that the people of any nation or language who say anything against the God of Shadrach, Meshach and Abednego be cut into pieces and their houses be turned into piles of rubble, for no other god can save in this way."'
> "Then the king promoted Shadrach, Meshach and Abednego in the province of Babylon" (Daniel 3:28-29).

Through the trials of these men, God had revealed His glory to a pagan nation and a righteous decree was passed throughout the provinces. For the storm earned Shadrach, Meshach and Abednego promotion in this life. That was the foretaste of the glory of the storm they went through.

Now read Daniel 6, the main focus of this point I am making here. Men had actually connived to set Daniel up. With all tact and wisdom, they got the king to pass an edict which barred prayers to any god. These men had no other way to get at Daniel except in a matter that concerned His God. May the world find no basis to get at us except for our faithfulness to God! May we really lead such blameless lives that whatever trap the devil sets, it shall be in vain!

So in defiance of the king's unrighteous decree, Daniel continued in his faithfulness, praying three times a day. As a result, he was thrown into the lion's den. But God sent His angels to shut the mouths of the lions. The king was overjoyed because actually he did not want to have Daniel killed. He had faith that Daniel's God would come to his rescue. Through this storm, Daniel saw God reveal Himself to a pagan nation and a righteous decree was again passed.

> *"Then King Darius wrote to all the peoples, nations and men of every language throughout the land: "May you prosper greatly! "I issue a decree that in every part of my kingdom people must fear and reverence the God of Daniel. For he is the living God and he endures forever; his kingdom will not be destroyed, his dominion will never end"* (Daniel 6:25-26).

The laws of God were now in force in a heathen nation, glory was brought to God. The storms brought Daniel material prosperity – a foretaste of the glories that come after the storms.

Storms Can Be Moments of God's Visitation

> *"He makes the clouds his chariot and rides on the wings of the wind"* (Psalm 104:3).

God actually uses clouds – moments of uncertainty to visit His people. They are chariots on which He mounts to visit His people. So when life seems very windy at times just lift up your head and watch for the appearing of your King, on a special visit to you. If there were no clouds around your life, on what will He mount? If there were no winds troubling your life, on what will He ride to come to you? So know this: sometimes God comes in the clouds. Do not ignore or despise such moments of God's visitation in your life.

Storms Come as Means Of Deliverance

> *"Has any god ever tried to take for himself one nation out of another nation, by testings, by miraculous signs and wonders, by war, by a mighty hand and an outstretched arm, or by great and awesome deeds, like all the things the LORD your God did for you in Egypt before your very eyes? You saw with your own eyes the great trials, the miraculous signs and wonders, the mighty hand and outstretched arm, with which the LORD your God brought you*

out. The LORD your God will do the same to all the peoples you now fear" (Deuteronomy 4:34, 7:19).

One way through which God worked out the deliverance of Israel was through the trials and testing they faced. They were not ordinary or little trials. The Bible terms them great trials. Actually when God passes you through great trials, He is working out a mighty deliverance for you from bondage either to sin, the devil, or some wrong habit. Storms at times come to deliver us from such things that will otherwise keep us bound. If you read Psalm 18, you will find that God came in the form of a mighty storm to save David from the claws of death. Again storms can be a means for your deliverance.

Peter said, *"He who has suffered has done away with sin"* (1 Peter 4:1). Suffering brings deliverance from sin. It comes to do away with our sinful desires and longings.

We can continue with the list of reasons why storms should come. So, learn to accept them, even as from the hand of God.

Chapter Sixteen

Facing the Storm

Now that we have seen the reasons why we should accept storms, if we should end there, then there is little that has been done. Surely you have asked, "How can I be helped to face the storms of my life?" This chapter and the next are dedicated just for that.

Arming Yourself

Storms are battles which Christians face in their lives in diverse ways. And in every battle, a man either comes out a victor or a victim. It is but true that he who goes into any battle unarmed is sure to meet everything but victory. Can you imagine a soldier going to war without a firearm or a bullet proof? Yet many of us get into storms unarmed. No doubt, instead of the supposed glory, storms bring us nothing but shame and defeat. Throughout scripture, I find only one instruction given to Christians to help them face suffering. It is simple but it works.

> *"Therefore, since Christ suffered in his body, arm yourselves also with the same attitude, because he who has suffered in his body is done with sin"* (1 Peter 4:1).

The first step to facing storms victoriously is to know that Christ suffered in His body. This prepares you psychologically and so you are sure that you are not alone in this way. What is happening to you happened to the One you now accept as your Lord, Savior, and King. And if you should follow in His footsteps then suffering must come.

The next step is to build a positive attitude toward the storm. Peter says, *"Arm yourself with the same attitude"*. In other words, your victory or defeat in moments of suffering depends totally on your attitude. If you put on a positive attitude and hope for the better, then you shall emerge victorious. Actually as a Christian, every battle you face is first of all gained or lost in the mind. This is the only arm you have at your disposal to face the storms with. Pick it up and use. If you ignore it, you are in for nothing but defeat.

Examples to Copy

> *"Brothers, as an example of patience in the face of suffering, take the prophets who spoke in the name of the Lord. [11]As you know, we consider blessed those who have persevered. You have heard of Job's perseverance and have seen what the Lord finally brought about. The Lord is full of compassion and mercy"* (James 5:10-11).

In his letter to God's suffering people across the globe, to help them face the storms they were going through, James called on them to consider as an example the prophets who spoke in the name of the Lord. He was telling them that they should know that this whole affair of suffering was for righteousness' sake. They were just part of such a large family of people who have lived across the generations. Now, He gave them a particular group of people to consider and take as an example. That we are going to do just here.

Already in this book, as an example in face of suffering, we have taken, Joseph, Job and prophet Jeremiah. Let's, for a moment, turn to the brief narrative of another prophet who went through tough times for the sake of righteousness.

Elijah The Tishbite

> "*Now Elijah the Tishbite, from Tishbe in Gilead, said to Ahab, "As the LORD, the God of Israel, lives, whom I serve, there will be neither dew nor rain in the next few years except at my word." Then the word of the LORD came to Elijah: "Leave here, turn eastward and hide in the Kerith Ravine, east of the Jordan. You will drink from the brook, and I have ordered the ravens to feed you there." So he did what the LORD had told him. He went to the Kerith Ravine, east of the Jordan, and stayed there*" (1 King 17:1-5).

In his days, there was so much idolatry and Baal worship that this prophet decided to command the rains to be withheld from the whole land. God, knowing the reaction of the king, commanded Elijah to go take refuge in the Kerith ravine. He was driven from home to live in the forest as a result of his righteous indignation against the sins of his land.

Maybe you are driven from that which rightfully belongs to you, because of your faith and belief. Maybe you are totally deprived of all that is called comfort for the sake of Christ. God says you should brave it up and draw strength from the examples, which are there in scripture to teach and encourage us.

I do not know the *"Ravine"* to which you have run for refuge but as long as the storms you endure are for righteousness sake, God will command ravens to take care of you. When a man moves out in faith at the command of God, all else is taken care of. The truth is that no matter how obscure your situation may be, God has not forgotten you. The God whom you serve will provide your needs in times of trouble. All you need do is to trust and to persevere. Thus from the examples of the prophets, God wants you to build up two things: patience and perseverance. Patience to keep you waiting for the day of God's deliverance and perseverance to keep you strong and unmoved by the storm! For "we consider blessed those who have persevered".

When the Mighty Fall

> *"Now Ahab told Jezebel everything Elijah had done and how he had killed all the prophets with the sword. So Jezebel sent a messenger to Elijah to say, "May the gods deal with me, be it ever so severely, if by this time tomorrow I do not make your life like that of one of them." Elijah was afraid and ran for his life. When he came to Beersheba in Judah, he left his servant there, while he himself went a day's journey into the desert. He came to a broom tree, sat down under it and prayed that he might die. "I have had enough, LORD," he said. "Take my life; I am no better than my ancestors." Then he lay down under the tree and fell asleep. All at once an angel touched him and said, "Get up and eat." He looked around, and there by his head was a cake of bread baked over hot coals, and a jar of water. He ate and drank and then lay down again. The angel of the LORD came back a second time and touched him and said, "Get up and eat, for the journey is too much for you." So he got up and ate and drank. Strengthened by that food, he traveled forty days and forty nights until he reached Horeb, the mountain of God. There he went into a cave and spent the night"* (1 King 19:1-9).

Have you felt like giving up lately? Have the storms been so persistent that you think the future holds nothing for you? Have you told the Lord that you have had enough of this stuff? Do you despair even of life? My brother, you are not alone. Even this mighty prophet, Elijah felt like giving up too. In fact, he asked the Lord to take away his life. A chapter before we read about the encounter between this mighty man of God and his God. We read of the assuring words of the Lord to him. We see in these lines the courage with which Elijah left Horeb to confront Ahab and now a message from Ahab's pagan wife sent him running for his life. Where had Elijah thrown his courage?

Do you find yourself in such a place? You do not feel like continuing this race any longer. At first you thought you were better than everybody else but now trouble has caused you to see that actually you are not better than anyone who has run the same race. At times suffering is a means of revelation. In it God shows you your true self; that you are nothing.

Chapter 16: Facing the Storm

When we reach the end of ourselves, God takes over. The Lord begins to work when you and I stop fighting. At the point of surrender, God refreshes us. God is saying to you, get up from your despair, receive strength and continue the journey. It is too early to give up. The journey is still too long for you. Continue to hold on, continue to persevere. God shall provide you with food from heaven that prepares you for the next phase of the journey.

With Christ in The Storm

In an earlier chapter, we talked of dangers to make sails without the Savior. We saw that every sail without Jesus is bound to meet storms. Does it mean that in every situation we face storms, Jesus is completely absent? Does it mean that when we move at His leadership our sail will be totally void of storms? We shall see in the next few lines that this is not the case. Even when we are sure that the Lord has commanded us to do something, there is every indication that His hand is in it, that His presence is actually with us, the storms shall still be there. Let's turn to another Bible narrative and draw from it a wealth of truths:

> *"Then he got into the boat and his disciples followed him. Without warning, a furious storm came up on the lake, so that the waves swept over the boat. But Jesus was sleeping. The disciples went and woke him, saying, "Lord, save us! We're going to drown!" He replied, "You of little faith, why are you so afraid?" Then he got up and rebuked the winds and the waves, and it was completely calm. The men were amazed and asked, "What kind of man is this? Even the winds and the waves obey him!"* (Matthew 8:23-27)

This is a sail authored by Lord Jesus. He led this journey and the disciples in loyalty followed their Master. Yet the Bible says, *"Without warning, a furious storm came up on the lake, so that the waves swept over the boat"*. The first truth we can learn from here is that, there are times and situations in which you sincerely follow the Spirit's leadership and yet meet the most horrible storms. But one thing should give you strength and confidence: He led you into it and that right there His presence is with you. No matter the storms battering your boat, as long as the Savior is there with you, nothing will happen to that boat.

Often, life's troubles and storms come without warning. They are often unforeseen and some will come with an increasing scale from mild to wild and still some will come with total fury as though to destroy you. At such moments, the ever present Lord seems silent as though wanting you to perish. Never give up calling on Him and knocking persistently on heaven's door until He answers and until the door is opened. With endurance, just look for your own position beside him in that same boat and lay you down in deep rest.

Do you remember David the night he fled from his son Absalom? When news was sent him that his own son was coming after him with a mighty army what did David do? The Bible says, *"I lie down and sleep, I wake again because the Lord sustains me"* (Psalm 3:5). How could he ever have slept in the center of such trouble? Was it worth bearing that risk? Yet because of his trust and confidence in his God, David could lie down and rest in God's protection.

At times, the silence of the Savior may mean that you use the command of faith to speak to your situation commanding things to normal. At times, the Lord can rebuke the storm for you. But this shall not always be so; He wants you to develop a strong faith and use the authority He has given you to speak to circumstances.

What if you call and there is no immediate response or you speak and the storms grow wilder? At such times, an altitude of trust in Him will be your strength, consolation, and hope. For it is certain that He who led you into the boat will not abandon you in the face of storms. Glory to His Name – our Rampart, Refuge, Horn and Shield! So, with Christ in the storm, you can always make it and take it no matter how hard it is. Thus, as God's chosen ones, you and I have something the world does not.

We have our Lord, Savior, and *"burden bearer"* willing to carry each of our burdens great or small. It is His good pleasure to see us roll onto Him our every care, worry, and anxiety. He wants to carry them for us. The sad thing is that many a saint wants to carry his or her burdens or problems. Unfortunately no one can carry his problems upon himself and enjoy sweet fellowship and communion with the Lord. Only one person is meant to be a burden bearer, the Man Jesus Christ.

There is one aspect in our fellowship with God, which we seem to miss; the aspect of rolling onto Him our every care. Listen once more to His invitation.

> *"Come to me, all you who are weary and burdened, and I will give you rest. Take my yoke upon you and learn from me, for I am gentle and humble in heart, and you will find rest for your souls. For my yoke is easy and my burden is light"* (Matthew 11:28-30).

As we said earlier, some misfortunes are indisputably as a result of sin or rebellion, while through others, God may just, in His sovereignty, decide to reveal His power and glory. We saw this somehow in the life of Job, how all his friends misinterpreted his misfortune as a consequence of his sin. But that was not the case, God just chose to reveal to principalities and powers, His glory through Job's situation. The Bible says,

> *"His intent was that now, through the church, the manifold wisdom of God should be made known to the rulers and authorities in the heavenly realms, ^{11}according to his eternal purpose which he accomplished in Christ Jesus our Lord"* (Ephesians 3:10-11).

Yeah! Through you and me, that is the church. Now let's turn to another Bible narrative to drive about this point

For the Display of His Power

> *"As he went along, he saw a man blind from birth. His disciples asked him, "Rabbi, who sinned, this man or his parents, that he was born blind?" "Neither this man nor his parents sinned," said Jesus, "but this happened so that the work of God might be displayed in his life"* (John 9:1-3).

There are certain things which God will allow to come your way not as a result of sin but that, through them, He may be glorified. Everything that happens to a believer independent of sin is a means to display and express God's infinite love, power, holiness, glory, and majesty; and make them manifest amongst men. Such is a result of God's working in His universe, in His church, or in a particular life. At times such workings will have the appearance of judgment for sin. It happened to this man, it happened to Job, and it has happened to countless people in the chronicles of Christian history.

It is always a heart pleasing sacrifice to God when His children rejoice that He is working through and in their lives. Again let it be written on your heart that what is happening to you as long as it is sin – independent, may be a means for God to display the riches of His blessing, His deliverance, His pardon, provision, or protection. You are His creature, He is sovereign (Romans 9:19).

A Strange Working

Take a look at John 9:6-11:

> *"Having said this, he spat on the ground, made some mud with the saliva, and put it on the man's eyes. "Go," he told him, "wash in the Pool of Siloam" (this word means Sent). So the man went and washed, and came home seeing. His neighbors and those who had formerly seen him begging asked, "Isn't this the same man who used to sit and beg?" Some claimed that he was. Others said, "No, he only looks like him." But he himself insisted, "I am the man." "How then were your eyes opened?" they demanded. He replied, "The man they call Jesus made some mud and put it on my eyes. He told me to go to Siloam and wash. So I went and washed, and then I could see"*
> (John 9:6-11).

Here we see that God has different methods of working for our good. Some may seem so foolish and harmful yet for our good. I wonder, don't you, how on earth to heal a blind man, Jesus would put mud on the man's eyes? Would this not have destroyed the man's eyes completely? Have you ever felt the pain

Chapter 16: Facing the Storm

of soil getting into your eyes? Biologically, what is the effect of soil in the eyes, but that it is destructive to sight? But here we see a total mystery that many of us could never come to grasp: how on earth applying mud – enemy to the eyes, healed bad eyes. In other cases, the Lord just spoke and others received their sight, why did He have to use mud in this case?

It is as though He was working against this blind man but praise God, He works in ways which will take us the whole eternity to comprehend if we ever would. At times when we expect Him to work in extraordinary ways, He resorts to simple but far reaching means. He uses ordinary means to accomplish the extraordinary. That is His strength, who can measure up to it? God's ways of working for your prosperity and success may just appear as though He is working for your ruin and failure. The truth is that in everything, God does His part and it is our responsibility to play ours.

He may have invested too much for your spiritual, financial or material prosperity. He may have done *"His part"* of the miracle, yet the most determinant and final step may depend solely on you. It may be just a little obedience without resistance, hesitation, complain or reservation. In the above passage, Christ had done all, the guy just needed to go to *"Siloam and wash"*. Had he disobeyed, he would have remained in abject blindness.

Is the misfortune you are facing a result of the fact that you refuse to go to your Siloam and wash? That may be where your breakthrough is. It may just be the point of your deliverance though it sounds foolish. Where is the "Siloam" God is sending you to? Please *"go and wash"*.

When he obeyed, his deliverance came, the *"storm of blindness"* was over, but a new storm started, that of rejection. Look, do not expect everybody to jump in glee when your breakthrough comes. There are people who are happy to see you stay in that misfortune but God is working out your deliverance in some way unknown to any man.

Maybe due to a breakthrough in an area of your life, you are facing rejection by your family, the society or the religious authorities, keep on to your faith in Christ. If you read through this story, you will find that this guy who received his healing put his faith in the One who healed him and immediately it was trouble for him. He was thrown out of the synagogue but Christ came and found him.

When men reject you, when men throw you out of their gathering because of acknowledgment of the truth, you will always fall in the arms of Jesus. He will always be there to accept you. The Lord will always move closer to assure and to reassure each time you hold unswervingly to the truth in the face of persecution and intimidation.

Jesus will always grant an extra revelation of Himself each time you hold steadfastly to the truth, proclaiming His love, power, and goodness, and declaring His justice. These will increasingly become your portion. This too is always granted; that in the face of storms, there is always the privilege of seeing Christ exalted and reigning as King. There is always a place in the arms of Jesus for those who refuse to conform to the lies and deceptions of Satan. There is always an extra favor to see more of Jesus, to know more of Him each time the standards are maintained. These are all the advantages of being with Christ in the storm.

Ignoring the Storm

Remember in this chapter we are talking of how we can face the storm, yet we are about to talk of ignoring the things we are supposed to face. That sounds funny or may be contradictory. But this is not so as we shall see. You see, some storms are not from God, though He may allow them. And often these come to distract and hinder you from concentrating on God and His purposes. As soon as you give attention to such, you realize there is no headway and every other thing becomes affected, for that was the purpose of the storm. At times all you need do is pay no attention to them. Keep your gaze and focus on Jesus and that which He has called you for and sooner or later you will realize that without any effort the storms have disappeared.

"Whoever watches the wind will not plant; whoever looks at the clouds will not reap" (Ecclesiastes 11:4).

If you watch some storms coming your way, man, you won't do anything reasonable. You won't invest or plant spiritually or even financially or materially. Ignore the wind and get on sowing your seed and the harvest shall be great. On the other hand, you may have sown, the fields are white and ripe but Satan causes the clouds to grow dark and as long as you look at the clouds you are afraid to harvest that which you have so much worked for. Man, ignore those dark clouds and go ahead and reap that which rightfully belongs to you. It is like allowing the distraction of a little child to deter you from something very important. Ignore the nuisance and it shall disappear when no attention is paid to it.

Set Your Heart on Pilgrimage

> *"Blessed are those whose strength is in you, who have set their hearts on pilgrimage. As they pass through the Valley of Baca, they make it a place of springs; the autumn rains also cover it with pools. They go from strength to strength, till each appears before God in Zion"* (Psalm 84:5-7).

There is a fountain of strength to face every storm unknown to many. It is the fact that we are on pilgrimage. The one who has set his heart on pilgrimage has nothing to worry about as far as prosperity in this world is concerned. He accepts what comes his way with relieve that it is just for a brief moment. Every child of God should put up with this attitude, it is a must. The one who fails to do so will suffer many pangs from failure and disappointments. The fact that you set your heart on pilgrimage reflects the fact that your strength lies in God alone and not in the success you achieve. Those whose heart are set on pilgrimage, *"As they pass through the valley of Baca, they make it a place of springs; the autumn rains also cover it with rains"*.

The valley of Baca is translated in the American Standard Version as *"the valley of weeping"*, and it means a situation of pain and sorrow. As they pass through this *"valley of weeping"*, they turn it to a place of joy and blessings. Those who set their heart on pilgrimage turn situations of weeping into moments of joy and blessings. They go from one level of strength to another on this pilgrim journey until they will appear before the Throne of God for their reward on that day of rewards. So those who set their heart on pilgrimage never grow weary. They move from strength to strength. To be better prepared to face storms, man set your heart on pilgrimage. Write it on your heart that your stay here is brief and that soon you will arrive your real home which is problem-free, and that will be for all eternity. Isn't that glorious?

Standing in the Storm

We have talked about arming yourself for storms and braving it out in the storms. Now like Paul said, *"Therefore put on the full armor of God, so that when the day of evil comes, you may be able to stand your ground, and after you have done everything, to stand"* (Ephesians 6:13)**.** I want to say here that *"Arm yourself, so that when the stormy days come, you may be able to face them, and after facing them, to stand"*. So it is not just facing the storms and falling after the storms are over but facing them and standing high even long after the storms are past. Have you seen a tree which was battered by storms and appeared to stand but immediately after the storms it crumbled to the ground? Such trees cause more havoc than if they had fallen during the storm because usually, after storms people are off guard. So here, we want to see how we can stand strong and high even after the storms have passed. The Lord Jesus Christ said,

> *"Therefore everyone who hears these words of mine and puts them into practice is like a wise man who built his house on the rock. The rain came down, the streams rose, and the winds blew and beat against that house; yet it did not fall, because it had its foundation on the rock. But everyone who hears these words of mine and does not put them into practice is like a foolish man who built his house on sand. The rain came down, the streams rose, and the winds blew and beat against that house, and it fell with a great crash"* (Matthew 7:24-27).

The secret to standing firm in the face of storms and long after the storms have passed is to practically live out the things of God, to practice the things which God reveals to you during your personal devotion. Usually God teaches and prepares us for everything before it happens to us, but only the one who puts these preparation lessons in practice benefit in any way from them.

1. The rain came down.
2. The stream rose
3. The winds blew and beat against.

These are all aspects of a storm and each has its own devastating effect upon the life of a man who faces them. If these things come upon a life unaffected, then such a life is invincible, why? Because it is built on the Rock. How? By living out, that is doing the word of God.

If you base everything you do on God's words, then man, you remain invincible or better still the house you are erecting is indestructible. The only confidence you and I have is that we act on the word of God. That is the only guarantee that in storms and even after the storms our work will continue to stand. If it rests on any other ground then it is sure to melt before the storms like wax melts before fire. So you have got to ask yourself "Is what I want to do based on the word of God? What is the foundation? On what will it stand?" if not when the rains come down, the streams rise and the winds blow and beat against that stuff, its destruction shall be great and complete.

Can you imagine the difference between the rock and sand when it comes to providing a foundation? What disparity! But this results from just one fact, the difference in attitude towards the word of God. One man takes it into consideration and another man neglects it. Again we see how important an armor our attitude is in the face of storms. Permit me ask you a question. What is your attitude towards the word of God? Are you a doer or just a hearer or reader? What about His personal words to you? Are they thrown away immediately afterwards or do you hold onto each stroke of it unswervingly with faith that it shall come to pass. What about the ones which demand not just faith but obedience? How do you take them?

Chapter Seventeen

God's Deliverance

We just concluded the chapter on *"facing the storms"*. We saw how we can arm ourselves, brave it out, and stand up in times of storms. But for how long can we stand? Only as long as God lends us strength! Were storms meant to be forever? Were you and I meant to remain in storms? Always facing it and braving it out and standing up to it? Surely for every storm God works out deliverance for you. He is working out one right now from the storms you are going through. So how can you cooperate with God to work out your deliverance? This chapter will try to bring just that out, to the least give an idea of what you should do and how God will always act on your behalf.

> *"For he who avenges blood remembers; he does not ignore the cry of the afflicted"* (Psalm 9:12).

That is it. God remembers your cries, your tears, your pain, your patience, your endurance, and He will not forget your cries – the cry of the afflicted. This means He will work out your deliverance and salvation even from the worst of it all.

Prepare the Way

When God wants to visit His people to bring about their deliverance, the way has to be prepared for Him to come. This is seen clearly in the ministry of John the Baptist. I already treated that in some detail in my book "Secret Exploits". Now for God to bring about your deliverance, you have to prepare His way. You may be wondering how on earth someone being battered by storms can ever have time to prepare God's way. Wait a minute!

> *"He who sacrifices thank offerings honors me, and he prepares the way so that I may show him the salvation of God"* (Psalm 50:23).

Normally, in times of distress, the average human tendency is to become anxious, complain and grumble. In the sight of God, this is sin and blocks His way to you. Maybe before we talk of decorating God's way, let us talk of how to keep barriers from His way, to totally keep away anything that will bar His way. This includes anxiety, worry, complaint, restlessness in any form, grumbling etc.

Now let's see how you can prepare His way.

"He who sacrifices thank offerings honors me and prepares the way..."

In order to prepare the way for your deliverance from storms, begin to give thank offerings. *"Oh God, I thank you for my life in spite of the fact that this is happening to me. Thank you that you permitted it. Thanks you for preserving my life in spite of the storms. I believe You will work it out for my good."* As you do that, you prepare His way to bring about your deliverance and salvation. It is for this reason that Paul said, *"Do not be anxious about anything, but in everything, by prayer and petition, with thanksgiving, present your requests to God"* (Philippians 4:6).

He also said, *"Be joyful always; pray continually; give thanks in all circumstances, for this is God's will for you in Christ Jesus"* (1 Thessalonians 5:16-18).

Chapter 16: God's Deliverance

As you give thanks, as you praise Him, the ancient gates are lifted up and the ancient doors swing open wide. The gate of brass and the bars of iron are broken and cut asunder. And the King of glory comes in with all power and mighty floodwaters to bring deliverance for His own. To better drive home this point, may we refer to the Bible narrative of Paul and Silas.

> *"After they had been severely flogged, they were thrown into prison, and the jailer was commanded to guard them carefully. Upon receiving such orders, he put them in the inner cell and fastened their feet in the stocks. About midnight Paul and Silas were praying and singing hymns to God, and the other prisoners were listening to them. Suddenly there was such a violent earthquake that the foundations of the prison were shaken. At once all the prison doors flew open, and everybody's chains came loose"* (Acts16:23-26).

Here we see Paul and Silas brutally flogged and thrown into the prison under special guard. As if that was not enough, they were transferred to an inner cell, legs placed in stocks and hands in chains. This is only a physical picture of how many a believer has been chained by the devil. Many like Lazarus are still with grave cloths and have to be unbound. Others are in serious chains, only one cannot tell how they ever got into it.

"About midnight..." Isn't that the time people are fast asleep? Isn't that the time *"our ancient foe doth seek to work his woe"* even in the life of the elect? That is why the singing and prayers of these missionary inmates had such sacrificial power. They were offering the sacrifice of praise to God at the time when only people who meant business could be awake to pray and sing praises.

Now why do praises prepare the way for God's salvation? This is because God inhabits, the praises of His people, He rides on our praises. As you sing praises to Him, you provide chariots for Him to mount. And when He mounts the chariot, the host of heaven comes along with Him and the spiritual realm is saturated with God's army. As victory is gained in the spiritual, the physical responds and results are seen. If you begin to praise God in that situation, those chains will begin to fall off. The doors will begin to swing open wide. Yeah, doors that were closed before you will begin to open and you shall enter a new realm of experience in your Christian life. Do you expect deliverance? Start offering thank offerings and making sacrifices of praise and your God will surely come.

God Would Make a Way

> *"I will make rivers flow on barren heights, and springs within the valleys. I will turn the desert into pools of water, and the parched ground into springs. I will put in the desert the cedar and the acacia, the myrtle and the olive. I will set pines in the wasteland, the fir and the cypress together, so that people may see and know, may consider and understand, that the hand of the LORD has done this, that the Holy One of Israel has created it"* (Isaiah 41:18-20).

> *"See, I am doing a new thing! Now it springs up; do you not perceive it? I am making a way in the desert and streams in the wasteland"* (Isaiah 43:19).

For how long have you been in the desert? For how long have you lived as though in a wasteland? God is about doing a new thing in your life. He is doing it already, can you perceive it? Can you sense the victory of your God in the spiritual? God is making a way out where there has been none. He is making a way into that blessing and fullness you have to enter. I perceive it strong in my spirit as I am writing. I do not know why but I sense God is doing a great thing for His people right now. He is making a high way across the desert, through the wastelands.

The thirst of His people will be satisfied and streams and springs are surfacing where there was none. Forget your former suffering and pain and agony and sorrow and begin to shout for joy, giving thanks for what God is about to do for His Church, for your life, your children, your parents, your relatives. God is making a high way for them into His Kingdom, into the fullness of His blessings.

In these two passages, we have something predominant coming up.

Chapter 16: God's Deliverance 155

1. Rivers of water on barren heights
2. Springs within the valley.
3. Pools of water in the desert
4. Springs from parched grounds
5. Streams in the wasteland

I believe the Spirit of God will be poured out upon His people in a mighty way like a river and He will make the difference in the Church of the First Born. The blessing He shall bring will be great and God's people shall be soaked in pools of spiritual and material fruitfulness. God is about to do things in your life, and it shall be evident to all that His own hand has done it. People will see and know, consider and understand that God is working in a mighty way through you and in you.

God's Salvation

We talked of you preparing the way, and of God making a way for your deliverance and salvation. While patiently waiting, trust that He will come, listen to His voice and wait for His deliverance. *"But those who suffer he delivers in their suffering; he speaks to them in their affliction. "He is wooing you from the jaws of distress to a spacious place free from restriction, to the comfort of your table laden with choice food"* (Job 36:15-16).

God is bringing your deliverance and now He is speaking to you in your affliction, only be keen enough to perceive that which He is saying to you. Be calm enough to hear the things He is communicating to you even in these trying moments. Your God wants to bring you to a spacious place; a place free from every kind of restriction or constraint; a place of freedom and comfort and varieties. That is the salvation God is bringing you. Do you believe that? Will you claim it?

> *"Strengthen the feeble hands, steady the knees that give way; say to those with fearful hearts, "Be strong, do not fear; your God will come, he will come with vengeance; with divine retribution he will come to save you"*
> (Isaiah 35:3-4).

Your God says, *"Be strong, do not fear"*. Strengthen those feeble hands, steady those knees which are knocking against each other. Look up with a steadfast hope and see your God coming. Do not lose your faith. Do not lose your trust, wait for Him.

> *"For the revelation awaits an appointed time; it speaks of the end and will not prove false. Though it linger, wait for it; it will certainly come and will not delay"* (Habakkuk 2:3).

His promises will not prove false, though it may tarry, though it lingers, wait for it. With certainty it shall come. With certainty He shall come and He shall save you. And like Habakuk, may you say,

> *"Though the fig tree does not bud and there are no grapes on the vines, though the olive crop fails and the fields produce no food, though there are no sheep in the pen and no cattle in the stalls, yet I will rejoice in the LORD, I will be joyful in God my Savior. The Sovereign LORD is my strength; he makes my feet like the feet of a deer, he enables me to go on the heights"* (Habakkuk 3:17-19*)*.

There may be no signs now of any improvement on your condition. All may still seem so dark and hopeless, no signs of God coming, but please rejoice, be joyful in God your Savior. For He alone is your strength and with Him, though all else should fail, you shall go on the heights. If there is one virtue I desperately need, it is patience and more and more, God is teaching me how to be still and wait patiently. May I quickly learn to wait patiently for God's salvation!

Rebuilding On The Ruins

What has been ruined in your life by the storms and calamity which have befallen you? Have you lost all to the wind or flames? All that can be seen now is the ruins and misfortunes. No strength to carry away the debris and all who pass by easily notice that a calamity passed through this man or woman's life. Each time you see the ruins, it reminds you of the horror of the storm that struck you and at each time, your heart pounds with fright, your lips quiver and decay seems to creep into your bones for you just cannot bear the sight of it. The LORD your God says to you, *"'But I will restore you to health and heal your wounds,' declares the LORD, 'because you are called an outcast, Zion for whom no one cares.' This is what the LORD says: 'I will restore the fortunes of Jacob's tents and have compassion on his dwellings; the city will be rebuilt on her ruins, and the palace will stand in its proper place'"* (Jeremiah 30:17-18).

God promises to restore you to your former position of glory and beauty in spite of all that has happened. He promises to heal the wounds, which the storms have caused in your life. What are the things you have lost? God is restoring them even now to you. Are they children? Is it money? Is it your reputation? Is it property? Is it your joy? Is it your peace? Is it your hope? Is it your trust? God says He will restore your fortunes and that they will be rebuilt on the ruins and stand in the place they are supposed to. Your enemies will see it and know that God is greater than all. In places where there are ruins He can erect wonders for His people. It is for you too, that you may see and believe that with Him all things are possible.

God's Everlasting Love

"Then maidens will dance and be glad, young men and old as well. I will turn their mourning into gladness; I will give them comfort and joy instead of sorrow. I will satisfy the priests with abundance, and my people will be filled with my bounty," declares the LORD. This is what the LORD says: "Restrain your voice from weeping and your eyes from tears, for your work will be rewarded "declares the LORD" (Jeremiah 31:13-14, 16).

God's love for you is everlasting. All He does is in His loving-kindness. Maybe you should take your Bible and read through Jeremiah 31. While you read, let the Spirit of God minister to your innermost being. I will not write much on God's love here. This subject is treated at length in my book "Child of God". But look at what He says He will do for you:

- You will dance and be glad
- You will be satisfied with abundance

- He will turn your mourning into gladness
- You will be filled with His bounty
- Your work will be rewarded

Men in Exchange for You

> *"But now, this is what the LORD says— he who created you, O Jacob, he who formed you, O Israel: "Fear not, for I have redeemed you; I have summoned you by name; you are mine. When you pass through the waters, I will be with you; and when you pass through the rivers, they will not sweep over you. When you walk through the fire, you will not be burned; the flames will not set you ablaze. For I am the LORD, your God, the Holy One of Israel, your Savior; I give Egypt for your ransom, Cush and Seba in your stead. Since you are precious and honored in my sight, and because I love you, I will give men in exchange for you, and people in exchange for your life. Do not be afraid, for I am with you"* (Isaiah 43:1-5[a]).

Why are we referring to flames and storms as *"flames and storms of glory"*? Because when we pass through them we are not consumed. Do you remember Moses in the "burning bush"? The forest was in flames but it was not consumed. This was nothing but God's glory. Here, God is speaking to you personally. Put your name everywhere you find Israel or Jacob and make it personal. God says fear not, you have been redeemed by the precious blood of His dear Son and so, He cannot afford to lose you. He says, you have been summoned by name. God has called you by your name and you are His forever.

When you pass through the waters, yeah the flood waters, the raging waters, He will be with you. When you pass through those rivers in life, which usually overflow their banks, they will not sweep over you. They will not carry you into the ocean. He says when you walk through the fire, the flames will not set you ablaze, you shall come out of it untouched. Why? Because He is the Lord your God and your Savior. My focus in this passage is verse 4:

> *"Since you are precious and honored in my sight, and because I love you, I will give men in exchange for you, and people in exchange for your life."*

Chapter 16: God's Deliverance

Have you ever been conscious of the fact that you are precious and honored in God's sight? Have you ever come to grips with that? God says because He loves you, He will give men in exchange for your life. So in times of trials, just keep cool. When men are plotting your ruin do not fight back, leave it in the hands of God. Let us look at some instances in brief.

In the case of Shadrach, Meshach and Abednego in Daniel 3, the soldiers were given in exchange for them.

In the case of Daniel and the Satraps of the kingdom of Persia, they thought they had worked out Daniel's downfall and destruction but God delivered him and *"At the king's command, the men who had falsely accused Daniel were brought in and thrown into the lions' den, along with their wives and children. And before they reached the floor of the den, the lions overpowered them and crushed all their bones"* (Daniel 6:24). The men were given in exchange for Daniel.

In the case of Peter and the guards, when God came to Peter's rescue, it is written *"In the morning, there was no small commotion among the soldiers as to what had become of Peter. After Herod had a thorough search made for him and did not find him, he cross-examined the guards and ordered that they be executed"* (Acts 12:18-19).

God is faithful. He shall keep to every promise of His. Glory to His awesome Name! Like in all these cases, you need not fight back. God will cause you to be a witness to the ruin that will befall your enemies. If you refuse to get even, God takes over and vindicates.

Chapter Eighteen

The Glory of the Storm

Hearing His voice

> *"These are the commandments the LORD proclaimed in a loud voice to your whole assembly there on the mountain from out of the fire, the cloud and the deep darkness; and he added nothing more. Then he wrote them on two stone tablets and gave them to me"* (Deuteronomy 5:22).

We have said that sometimes God comes in the clouds when visiting His people. In this example it is said that God spoke to the assembly out of

1. The fire.
2. The cloud
3. The deep darkness.

What does fire bring but heat and pain? What do the clouds bring but rain and sometimes lightning? So too is deep darkness. All these bring along only discomfort and fright but the good thing is that out of them God speaks. Often, we so respond to the pain, fright, and discomfort these come along with that our ears become closed up to the voice of God speaking out of them. In such a situation, where God comes in storms, all you need do is to keep your patience. Hold your peace and stay cool. Trust and believe that God is there and tune your spirit to heaven's frequency.

How often has He spoken and we do not hear Him because of worry and anxiety. Lift up your eyes beyond the clouds and darkness and you shall behold your God and your Father. In the heat of the fire which surrounds you, God is there. In the thundering of the clouds over your head God is there. In the deep darkness which apparently engulfs you, God is right there with you. Though you may question the pain, though you may in your mind wonder why God has abandoned you, know that He has not. He is in the process of shaping the pearl so precious to Him for His glory and yours too.

So in all the noise that surrounds you, you can always hear God's still small voice of direction, of comfort, of love and of hope.

The Crown of Life

> *"Blessed is the man who perseveres under trial, because when he has stood the test, he will receive the crown of life that God has promised to those who love him"* (James 1:12).

> *"Do not be afraid of what you are about to suffer. I tell you, the devil will put some of you in prison to test you, and you will suffer persecution for ten days. Be faithful, even to the point of death, and I will give you the crown of life"* (Revelation 2:10).

Perseverance is a blessing from God. The one who perseveres is blessed. If there were no trials where would perseverance come from? All who love God are bound to come under severe trials and testing to prove the authenticity of their love, and one of the greatest tests of authenticity is time. True and authentic love stands the test of time even in trials.

Love for God is proven true by the willingness (not ability) to stand trials for His sake. God in His wisdom has made it in such a way that only those who persevere receive the reward, yeah those who go through all of the tests. And

Chapter 18: The Glory of the Storm

trials are there to do just that – test us and prove us worthy of the reward of God. And this reward is for he who *"has stood the test"*.

1. There is no reward for he who stands a little of the test.
2. There is no reward for he who stands half of the test.
3. There is no reward for he who stands most of the test.
4. There is no reward for he who stands almost all of the tests.

The one and only reward – The crown of life – is for he who has stood the entire test. So as you stand in the storms, this should be your comfort that a reward awaits you - *"The crown of life"*. Maybe we should call it *"the crown of everlasting life"*. Oh! What bliss should fill your soul, what comfort, what hope! Besides, God's end-time promises are for the overcomer. Just take a look at them:

1. Right to eat from the tree of life (Revelation 2:7).
2. No hurt by the second death (Revelation 2:11).
3. Be given hidden manna and a white stone with a new name on it (Revelation 2:17).
4. Authority over all nations (Revelation 2:26).
5. Dressed in white (Revelation 3:5).
6. Be made a pillar in the temple of God (Revelation 3:12).
7. Right to sit on His throne (Revelation 3:21).

What glories await those who pass through trials and who stand through perseverance and trust in God! See trials and storms as tests which come to make you partake of the sufferings of Christ thus be rendered worthy to partake of His glory. Your commitments to God will be tested by storms and flames. Your obedience to God will be tested by storms and flames. Your love for God will be tested by storms and flames. Your faith in God will be tested by storms and flames. And that which is true and authentic will stand the test. That which is false and counterfeit will fail the test at some stage. So hold on: neither give up nor give in. Lift your head and see *"the eternal glories that gleam afar to nerve your faith endeavor"*.

Eternity's Perspective

> What are your fears?
> What are your pains?
> What are your weaknesses?
> What are your limitations?
> What are your failures?
> What are your cries?
> What are your lacks?
> What are your sorrows?
> What are your worries?

Maybe you should list down the answers to each question. Now address each of them and speak to them. Tell them they are just for a brief moment, in eternity they shall not be there. For when the Lord shall come, they shall all be dealt away with, conquered forever.

Now,

> What are your desires?
> What are your longings?
> What are your passions?
> What are your needs?

Again, you may want to list them down and speak to them that each one of them will be met. When you see Him you shall become like Him.

Our hope and our home are all beyond the sky. Though we may receive a foretaste here on earth, the "real thing" is in eternity. That is why Paul could say,

> *"If only for this life we have hope in Christ, we are to be pitied more than all men"* (1Corinthians 15:19).

> *"Listen, I tell you a mystery: We will not all sleep, but we will all be changed— in a flash, in the twinkling of an eye, at the last trumpet. For the*

> trumpet will sound, the dead will be raised imperishable, and we will be changed. For the perishable must clothe itself with the imperishable, and the mortal with immortality."
>
> "Therefore, my dear brothers, stand firm. Let nothing move you. Always give yourselves fully to the work of the Lord, because you know that your labor in the Lord is not in vain" (1 Corinthians 15:51-53, 58).

Understanding God's Attitude

> *"This is what the LORD says: "Let not the wise man boast of his wisdom or the strong man boast of his strength or the rich man boast of his riches, but let him who boasts boast about this: that he understands and knows me, that I am the LORD, who exercises kindness, justice and righteousness on earth, for in these I delight," declares the LORD"* (Jeremiah 9:23-24).

Well, certainly much has been said with respect to us. It will be unfair to end this study without letting you know God's attitude towards you. God wants you to understand and know Him as One who;

1. Exercises kindness.
2. Exercises justice.
3. Exercises righteousness

When you know and understand God in such ways, He takes delight in you. If you understand Him as a God who exercises kindness, you will rest assured that in everything He is in absolute control and that all He does is part of His kindness and justice and righteousness. Every act of God consists of all three and if you see it thus, you will flow out always in thanks and adoration.

He Longs to Be Gracious to You

> *"Yet the LORD longs to be gracious to you; he rises to show you compassion. For the LORD is a God of justice. Blessed are all who wait for him! O people of Zion, who live in Jerusalem, you will weep no more. How gracious he will be when you cry for help! As soon as he hears, he will answer you"*
> (Isaiah 30:18-19).

God is not indifferent to what is happening to you. He is not indifferent to your frustration. He is not indifferent to your needs and to all that causes you pain and tears. He sees them all, He knows them all, He longs to be gracious to you, to show you His kindness and goodness. The problem is that at times we do not give Him the chance due to much worry. God longs to show you His favor, He longs to be part of that circumstance, to feel the pains you feel, to wipe away your tears. He rises to show you compassion. He is taking the necessary steps to help. His heart is full of pity due to your sufferings. He wants to share your suffering. Maybe your situation is as a result of His justice but that same justice compels Him to show compassion. The secret is to wait for Him; to wait in repentance and rest and in quietness and trust, where the strength to endure lies.

You may ask, *"when will all this happen?"* His word gives you the response; *"As soon as He hears He will answer you"*. And *"when will He hear?"* You may say! Well "when you cry for help!" Have you cried for help? How many have cried due to self-pity, cries of regret and cries of failure but hardly any cry for help. Many weep and weep but never cry for help. All we do at times is wish help would come or we ask for help, but how I wish we would cry and cry out loud for God's help. Crying usually shows how desperate a man may be and how urgent help is needed. God will show you favor when you cry for help. Remember what God told Moses:

> *"The LORD said, "I have indeed seen the misery of my people in Egypt. I have heard them crying out because of their slave drivers, and I am concerned about their suffering. So I have come down to rescue them from the hand of the Egyptians and to bring them up out of that land into a good and spacious land, a land flowing with milk and honey—the home of the Canaanites, Hittites, Amorites, Perizzites, Hivites and Jebusites. And now the cry of the Israelites has reached me, and I have seen the way the Egyptians are oppressing them"* (Exodus 3:7-9).

Do you see that? *"I have heard them crying out ... and I am concerned about their suffering"*. And *"and the cry of the Israelites has reached me..."* Your cry will arouse His concern. Oh no! God is already concerned about you, about your suffering, about your misery (Exodus 3:25). Tears have power, but how little do we realize it. I am referring to the right tears. Like little children let us learn to cry out to our God.

> *Jeremiah said, "The hearts of the people cry out to the Lord. O wall of the Daughter of Zion, let your tears flow like a river day and night; give yourself no relief, your eyes no rest. Arise, cry out in the night, as the watches of the night begin; pour out your heart like water in the presence of the Lord. Lift up your hands to him for the lives of your children, who faint from hunger at the head of every street"* (Lamentations 2:18-19).

Yeah! Give yourself no relief until He has heard and answered. Remember I said we have to understand and know God also as a God of justice. He will not fail to exercise His justice. Why? Because He will not share His glory with any man (Isaiah 48:11, 42:8). As a Father, He merits our total attention and dependence. You see, many times the sufferings we go through is because we seek help from the wrong places and often this brings disgrace to our God. Think of it, if you have a son or daughter who is in need and instead of telling you, he runs to your enemy to ask for help. Will you be happy? Will you be happy that after having told him to wait, he becomes impatient and runs to your enemy to seek for help. It is the same thing we do yet we take it lightly.

> *He says, "Woe to those who go down to Egypt for help, who rely on horses, who trust in the multitude of their chariots and in the great strength of their horsemen, but do not look to the Holy One of Israel, or seek help from the LORD. Yet he too is wise and can bring disaster; he does not take back his words. He will rise up against the house of the wicked, against those who help evildoers. But the Egyptians are men and not God; their horses are flesh and not spirit. When the LORD stretches out his hand, he who helps will stumble, he who is helped will fall; both will perish together"* (Isaiah 31:1-3).

Is the reason for your sorrow, affliction and calamity your going to the world to seek help? He has promised grief for anyone who seeks help or relies on anything apart from Him. He is committed to take away anything you look up to, everything you rely on, everything you seek help from. He is committed to have all of your attention and nothing will stop Him. His glory is that His children look up to Him and Him alone. When you begin depending on anything or anyone else, then you are expecting Him to share His glory with another, a thing He will never do. God is the only One who never fails. So if what you are going through is a result of your unholy alliances, then you better repent before calamity comes in full (see Isaiah 30:1-3, 2 Chronicles 20:35-37). No matter what the loss may be, decide to gain God's favor (2 Chronicles 25:1-10).

As we seek to trust and wait, may we out of every stony grief raise a Bethel and with the hymn writer sing, "out of my stony grief, Bethel I'll raise"

What about His Promises

Has God spoken to you about something of your future? Are you taking it to heart? Have you *"waited for too long"*? Let us end our book with this assurance that God's promises shall come to pass. *"But I don't have faith or trust"* You may say, *"God's promises are for those with mighty faith to storm God's store house and bring His promises to pass"*. Well. If that is what you think, wait a minute, and let me show you something from God's word.

> *"¹Now the LORD was gracious to Sarah as he had said, and the LORD did for Sarah what he had promised. ²Sarah became pregnant and bore a son to Abraham in his old age, at the very time God had promised him. ³Abraham gave the name Isaac to the son Sarah bore him. ⁴When his son Isaac was eight days old, Abraham circumcised him, as God commanded him. ⁵Abraham was a hundred years old when his son Isaac was born to him"* (Genesis 21:1-5).

You see, God is committed to fulfill every promise made by Him to His own. He does what His lips utter. He honors His words. The Bible says,

> *"God is not a man, that he should lie, nor a son of man, that he should change his mind. Does he speak and then not act? Does he promise and not fulfill?"* (Numbers 23:19)

> When He speaks, He acts.
> When He promises, He fulfills.
> He does not change His mind.

Our reference in Genesis tells us that;

1. *"The Lord was gracious to Sarah as He had said"*.
   Our God is not one who says one thing and does another. He is a God of truth. What He has said to you, He will do. Nothing can ever change that.

2. *"The Lord did for Sarah what He had promised"*.
   God always fulfills His promises. There are absolute promises of God independent of the object of His promise. In spite of you, God will fulfill His promise. "But Sarah was a woman of faith", you say. Well, maybe. But we are talking about a Sarah who doubted God, a Sarah who laughed when God spoke, one to whom all what God said seemed to be without meaning, for that was the meaning of her laughter (see Genesis 18:11-15). That is the Sarah for whom God fulfilled His promise.

"But the promise was to Abraham the man of faith", you say, *"And I have no credit ever given me as a result of my faith"*. Again to you I say this, we are talking about Abraham who doubted God, one who laughed and asked questions of unbelief (Genesis 17:17-20), who could not see beyond Ishmael. God saw Isaac, Abraham saw Ishmael. Oh that each of us would persistently ask God *"Lord what do you see about my future? I can only see as far as Ishmael – the evidence around but I know you have an Isaac for me"*.

Though Abraham's faith had dwindled, God still fulfilled His promise. Does that give you hope?

3. *"... at the very time God had promised"*.
   God is never late. He is a God who keeps time. Many a time, we do not seek to know for what time or period God had made a cer-

tain promise. We often think God is in the same time frame with us and in our anxiety to see it fulfilled we think time is running out. God is not an opportunist that circumstances should force Him to act. He creates the situation to suit His program. God will fulfill His promise the very time He has said. You need just wait and be patient and trust. (Isaiah 30:15).

"But I blew it up already", you say! Maybe out of impatience you blew it up and *"Your Hagar"* has brought forth an Ishmael. It happened with Abraham (then Abram). He could not wait and so decided to bring forth a family for Sarah (then Sarai) through Hagar (Genesis 16:2). Sarah was so interested in making a family for herself. If your impatience has brought an Ishmael in your life, do not despair. Just ask for God's forgiveness. Do not insist that God blesses your Ishmael for that very thing may turn out to be a thorn and hindrance to what God wants you to become. Look beyond your Ishmae*l "to the Isaac"* God has for you. I do not know how many times you *"blew it up"*, God's Isaac will come. Only, do not insist that your Ishmael become a nation for you shall live to regret it.

> *"Sarah said, "God has brought me laughter, and everyone who hears about this will laugh with me." And she added, "Who would have said to Abraham that Sarah would nurse children? Yet I have borne him a son in his old age"* (Genesis 21:6-7).

God is about to make you laugh. All this while you probably have been crying but God wants to make you laugh and friends who have mocked you will laugh with you. Oh God, bring laughter to your children; to aching hearts which have been groaning; to individuals whose faces are flooded with tears of pain; to those whose hope can only reach their Ishmael. Yes Lord, for laughter makes the heart merry. Do it for your own Name's sake, Amen!"

But remember when the promise was fulfilled, Abraham had to fulfill certain conditions for the promise to continue. The *"first phase"* was in spite of Abraham, (the birth of Isaac) but the part of becoming the father of many nations depended on him. He had to fulfill his side of the covenant.

- Naming the child Isaac
- Circumcising the child

In the laughter, God has given you do not forget Him.

Glory to God in the highest!

Chapter Nineteen

A Friend's Testimony

Bellville, 10th December 2003.

"Yes I have loved you with an everlasting love, and I have been your shelter, and I will watch over you. Yes for good. I will not abandon you. Yes I know you. Yes my name is the Lord, my love is unbounded, my love is unbounded. I have loved you and I will love you always. Yes I am the Lord your God who watches over you. Even when you pass through the fire, I will be there. Be not afraid, I am the lord your God who watches over you."

This was the word of prophecy at the CMFI student assembly Praise and Worship service on Sunday the 16th of June 2002. It was in the same light with what God had been ministering to the student body all through that week. The Holy Spirit was carrying out a deep ministry of encouragement, spurring us to look up to Him and believe His word and trust in His promises never to leave or forsake us. To be with us always, even to the end of time. Beginning Friday 14th at the Prayer meeting, we had been reading from the book of Isaiah 43:1-4, which says, *"...Fear not, for I have redeemed you; I have summoned you by name; you are mine. When you pass through the waters, I will be with you; and when you pass through the rivers, they will not sweep you over. When you walk through the fire, you will not be burned; the flames will not set you ablaze. For I am the Lord, the holy one of Israel, your savior; I give Egypt for your ransom, Cush and Seba in your stead..."* (NIV).

We also had been examining the passage of the disciples at sea with the Lord Jesus during the storm. We realized that as long as Jesus was in the boat, there was no way it was going to sink. We imagined the disciples should have known Jesus enough to realize that nothing could befall them as long as he was with them in that boat. We also examined the contrastive reaction of the Lord Jesus in the boat, who had so much peace that He could even sleep. The Holy Spirit was ministering to us that in our walk with the Lord, there will sometimes be storms and moments of trials. God never said it was just going to be a bed of roses, he only promised to be there with us in those moments. He promised to be with us through the fire and through the rivers, to make sure they don't set us ablaze and the floods don't cover us respectively.

Through song, prayer and worship, the Holy Spirit enabled me to lead the Sunday service, fully convinced that he was there to minister this message in a personal way to whoever needed to grasp it. It had been laid so heavily on my spirit as I prepared to lead the service. Little did I know that God granted me to prepare the message first hand, because I was going to need it the most. So as the service ended that faithful Sunday, I noticed that a senior uncle of mine had tried to get me by phone at a time when he knew I would be in church. I immediately knew it was not a courtesy call.

My mind began to pace as I made efforts to figure out what could have gone wrong back home. As I moved along the lonely path that led to my student room, a sense of peace came over my spirit and I made a prayer to God, I thanked him for deciding to pass me through the fire and I prayed that he would be there with me and help me through the trial that lay ahead of me. I eventually got the phone call that confirmed my fears and began a period I would describe as the 'most trying moment of my life'. Of all the possibilities I thought of, my father with whom I lived in the same town, whom I had last seen on Tuesday 11th and he had promised to come visit my sister and I over the weekend, had been killed in a ghastly motor accident, in another town so many kilometers from where we lived.

This had actually taken place on Friday 14th and he had died on Saturday 15th but I was only getting the news on Sunday. Needless to say this was a real shock to me. He had not told me of any plans to travel, besides losing someone in the heart of my final exam was not the best thing to have happened to me. I had just written one course. I had two more courses to go and my end of course dissertation to complete. How was I going to concentrate, knowing that my father was lifeless in a fridge somewhere? Besides the pain of losing a loved one, the path we had come as a family made this state of affairs difficult to accept.

Coming from a polygamous family, my father had separated from my mother when I was 10 years old. I was quite fond of him when we lived together and I loved him very deeply. After the separation, we never saw each other for over four years, time during which he married the woman he had left my mother for. These years of separation were difficult ones for us. There were times when we couldn't come to buy decent food to eat. We got kicked out of the house we were renting because my mother could not meet up with the financial burden of maintaining my brother and I in college and keeping pace with other financial responsibilities. We packed our household items into a store and moved in with a Christian family, who lovingly offered the only other room in their house for the three of us to occupy. This had been a move from grace to grass, time during which we came to know the Lord Jesus Christ.

I had a reasonably modest childhood, which sharply contrasted the situation I was going through at that moment. But God was faithful to me, he caused me to maintain my concentration at school and still make my exams. It is difficult to see your mother suffer and be indifferent towards whoever you believe is responsible. We knew, or believed, my father was operating under some kind of a spell from his new wife and so we prayed for him relentlessly and begged the Lord to bring him back to us. But as we prayed and hoped for the best, the years passed and the separation was maintained. Passing from High School to University finally offered me the opportunity of living with him again in the same town after seven years since he had left us.

A new relationship was born between us. This for me was a chance to make up for the lost years. I had placed aside the hurt of the years of separation and was out for a new beginning. I still loved him deeply and came to realize that he loved me too and had also been feeling the pain of the lost years. We became great friends, with him treating me as a grown up and from time to time taking care as a father that he was. We returned to the things we used to do together as a family, went to the military club to play tennis and other fun walks. I took my position of son and took care of his house, cleaning and at times cooking for him, preparing his shoes as I had done at the age of seven. Coming close to him, made me realize how miserably he lived.

In spite of the handsome salary package, his apartment was less furnished than my little student room in every respect. But I hoped for the best. I was on a good course at the university, and was determined to change the predicament of my father as soon as I had the means. I dreamt of better days and trusted God for a time when it will seem like it had only been a dream. We had come to grips with the mistakes of the past and were both looking ahead, to a bright future.

That *'last Tuesday'*, we had been examining my university transcripts and doing what he had been fond of doing since our new found relationship, a countdown to my graduation day. I saw in a man beaten by life's struggles a glimmer of hope, something to look up to, a reason to rejoice, and I was determined to give him that pleasure. It was going to be great joy moving into the graduation ceremonial ground to take pictures with his son and later on invite his friends to a reception in the evening and have something to be proud of.

To think that an event we had looked forward to for the three years that we had been together, was going to take place without him, gave me an additional reason to weep. True or typical of my extended family history, it was believed he had died a mysterious death, in a month during which it has been observed, at least a family member had died in the past many years. So his death appeared not to be a surprise to some, it was like anticipated. Their behavior sent a message like, 'that serves him right'. Typical of their traditional customs or due to their knowledge of the happenings or out of share insensitivity, his family treated us very poorly during the preparations, during and after his burial. But God kept his promises to me. He gave me strength to face each of these circumstances. He provided all the financial and material needs for the burial. He raised his children to share our pain and to take care of each of us with special attention. Indeed it was like passing through the fire, but it did not set me ablaze. That he was there through the fire did not make the fire cease from being fire, it burnt and it hurt, it was painful and difficult to accept. He was passing me through a process of purification in the furnace. Through it all, I am thankful today that he has healed me deeply and continues to do so every day. I learnt a number of lessons that constituted my healing process and facilitated the transformation of my trial into a testimony for his glory.

First of all, true to his word, the Lord was with me and acted in such faithfulness that it was evident it could only be Him at work. Beginning with my exams, He showed Himself faithful. In spite of a malaria attack during my final paper, I obtained my best grades at the university during that semester. He gave me A's in three of my five courses including my end of course dissertation. I came to understand that as a child of God, there is nothing that happens to you that takes God unawares. It has become my frequent consolation in the face of unexpected happenings. I just tell myself, I may be surprised at this, but this has not taken God by surprise. He has everything well figured out. Before He decides to bring us through any situation, He has figured out all the possibilities and concluded that it was the best way to get the thing done. He then takes the necessary moves to enable us go through the trial.

Being at a crossroad in my life, I was challenged to trust God with my future. To believe that as He says, He is a God of the widows and orphans. Just completing a degree and losing a parent brought moments of doubt and uncertainty to me. The month following the release of my first degree results, I applied and was offered a provisional admission into a school in Britain, subject to the payment of some pre-inscription fees. I almost immediately began to feel the impact of my dad's absence. Overwhelmed by the pressure of the recent happenings and motivated by the desire to move out of the too much pressure that I was under, I made every possible effort to get this fee paid. It was not an amount too big, but for some reason it was not coming my way. I paced through different towns and contacted influential people asking for assistance, but none was ready to do anything for me. I felt stupid in front of some of these people whom I had barely introduced myself to and expected them to take financial commitments on my behalf. But that was how hard I tried and fought.

The deadline passed and I retreated from my search and returned home. This was a dark moment for me. I felt like all else was against me. There were times when I felt like the air around my head had weight, I mean literally heavy. I was at the end of myself. I told myself, if my father were alive, he would not have let such an opportunity pass by. He had some savings that were equivalent to my required fee and I knew he would have done all he could to make me study abroad. I asked God many questions. In the process I grew angry, very angry with the people who to me had made life this miserable for me and my family. This same people had proceeded to a different phase of action. Beyond the confusion they had engineered in my father's life, they were determined to continue to make life difficult for us after his death.

We (my brothers and sisters) fell out with his brothers and wife through some spirit of confusion that was difficult to understand. They made every possible effort to prevent us from having access to whatever financial packet that could have been useful to us at such a moment. The various savings and contributions they collected in his name including his salary disappeared into thin air. They were spent in organizing inappropriate luxurious ceremonies at a time when I, my brothers and sisters needed money to go back to school. The fact that they did not take our interest to heart made me angrier and intensified my pain. But God preserved me during those moments from acting upon my pain and anger.

There were times when I wished I could separate myself from my Christian identity and stage a real war for survival, but I had to learn to fight the battle God's way. He says we do not wrestle against flesh and blood and though we live in the world, we don't wage war as the world does. The urge to fight back was strong. There were times I had this urge to go and set everything on fire: the car they were fighting over and the house being built in the village. I desired to get the world know my frustration and pain. I was looking for an appropriate way to vent out my anger. But God was merciful to me and he did not let me do anything foolish.

Stopping the fight and releasing myself and my whole family to the Lord was the key to my healing process. Literally put, I was led to let everything in God's hands. I had come to the end of myself, to the end of seeking for a solution. I had not given up on life, I only accepted my situation, committed my life into God's hands and hoped for his intervention. I was being prepared for a new beginning and a fresh start. Apart from letting God fight this battle, I had the obligation to forgive all those who had hurt my family and me and release them to God. There were difficult steps to take but God gave me the leading and boldness to take those steps.

Digging through my father's files, I came across letters that revealed the turbulent nature of his relationship with his new wife. They contained puzzling details we had this far not understood. Deep revelations about situations my father had been going through in the last years of his life. The least I can say about them here is that they could have made forgiveness for the perpetrators difficult to anyone who truly loved my father. But I made a covenant of forgiveness with the Lord. I told God, I am forgiving and releasing these people to you. I burnt the letters and once and for all destroyed any physical evidence of the wrongs done to my father and family. I was taking, by this act, the initiative to close the doors to resentment and animosity.

The worst had happened, but it was time to move on and to move ahead. It certainly was not the easiest thing to do, but it had to be done. It would have been a double tragedy for me to come out of the pain and be locked up in the dungeon of bitterness. I prayed very hard against this. I reminded God I knew I was supposed to forgive and to release and to get on. I told him I found that hard to do, but I wanted to do it because I realized it was the right thing to do. This opened me up further to the move of God and the beginning of His healing process in my heart.

After my graduation, I moved back to my university town and began a job search. It was like coming out of a long nightmare and waking up to start life all over. There was still much evidence of a wound in my heart, but God was healing it and speedily too. I prepared and dropped applications for a job in various companies, but I did not receive any a call for an interview. But God had a master plan in mind. During this period, many of my classmates were picking up jobs all around me and I sometimes asked God if I was going to be the last. I must however confess that this period of waiting was one of the most spiritually enhancing times of my life. I found myself in a group of young and committed believers and we busied ourselves in telling the other students about Jesus. I also had the chance to be around my kid brother and sister and to build a loving relationship with them and the rest of my sisters who lived in the same town. We were an encouragement to each other and helped each other develop a positive outlook on life and a hope for a better future. We found a new unity in the pain we jointly shared.

I later found a job as a stores accountant for a small gift shop and a bakery owned by one man. My duties at the bakery were not well defined and I sometimes extended my functions to the delivery of bread with the bread van to our various clients in different locations. This was very humbling for someone with my qualification, but I knew though it appeared I had hit the bottom of life, I was in for a rise. My job taught me the little discipline of being answerable to a boss and kept me busy, besides the discipline of waking and going out early to work. I did not make much money, but just enough to take care of myself and one or two needs.

A month afterwards, I picked up a contract as an administrative assistant to one of my lecturers at the university. I had short and flexible working hours and a career enhancing training. I had a slightly higher pay package and a lot of fringe benefits and remunerations. This job was a real blessing to me. I had begun to taste of the choice provisions of the Lord. This was only a beginning because from every indication, the Lord was determined to wipe off our tears. This gave me first hand access to any administrative recommendation and document that I could have required from the university.

I was where God wanted me to be and He showed me enormous favors in many respects. He provided faithfully for my siblings to go back to school and showed us enormous favors at various levels. Not once did we have to borrow to meet up with any urgent need. There was always a provision for each situation. With the little savings that I had started building, I was able to complete and post an application file for a scholarship to study for a Master program at a university in Cape Town, South Africa, from where I am writing this testimony. The Lord blessed me with a full scholarship that covered my flight to and from Cape Town, tuition, accommodation and a Living allowance. No job back home could have given me the level of satisfaction I now have doing a Master program. My mother remarked that the scholarship I received was an endowment from some rich person's legacy to promote education. In a way, God was giving more from some other person's legacy, what I couldn't get out of my own father's legacy.

I send this testimony out of a heart of gratitude for all that the Lord Jesus has been to me. I am humbled to testify of his goodness to my family and me. God is a God that sees the end from the beginning and calls things that are not as if they were. He equips us adequately to face the things He allows to come our way. The moments may be really painful and trying for us, but it is important that we be still and believe that His plans for us are the best. He says, *"… No eye has seen, no ear has heard, no mind has conceived what God has prepared for those who love him. But God has revealed it to us by his spirit. The spirit searches all things, even the deep things of God"* (1 Corinthians 2:9-10). My prayer for myself and whoever reads this testimony is that we may be brought to understand the depth of God's wisdom and love for his children. No mind may be able to conceive it, but God promises to reveal it to us through the Holy Spirit that searches the deep things of God. This should be our encouragement in the face of trials and hardship: to know that they are only temporary and at the end of it all, the Lord achieves for us a glory that makes us forget the days of our bitterness of Soul.

Conclusion

In conclusion...

I believe you have been blessed by the teachings and testimony in this book. This book was written back in 2003, and many years have passed since then. My friends went on to obtain his Master's Degree and has held numerous Jobs since then. Of course he is married and a father of three.

Whatever you go through, remain faithful to your God and to His word and every storm or flame will lead you to glory. I invite you to establish a solid relationship with the Lord Jesus and live fully for God and His Kingdom.

Other publications from the publisher

Other publications from the publisher

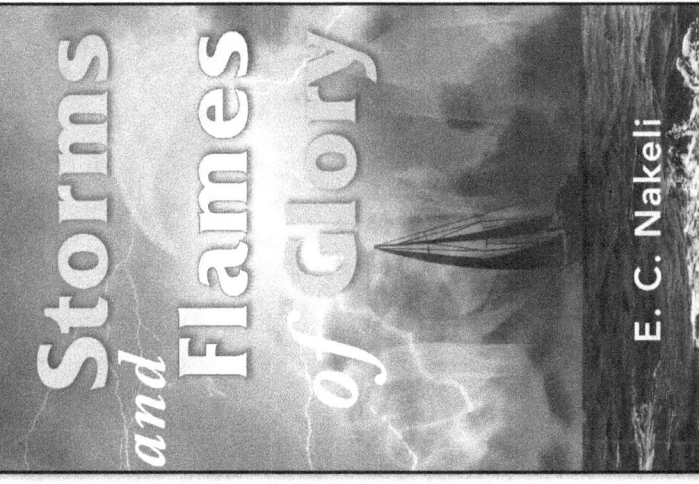

Other publications from the publisher

Other publications from the publisher

www.ingramcontent.com/pod-product-compliance
Lightning Source LLC
Chambersburg PA
CBHW071617080526
44588CB00010B/1159